BEYOND DIVORCE CASUALTIES

BEYOND DIVORCE CASUALTIES

Reunifying the Alienated Family

Douglas Darnall, Ph.D.

TAYLOR TRADE PUBLISHING
Lanham • New York • Boulder • Toronto • Plymouth, UK

Published by Taylor Trade Publishing
An imprint of The Rowman & Littlefield Publishing Group, Inc.
4501 Forbes Boulevard, Suite 200, Lanham, Maryland 20706
http://www.rlpgtrade.com

Estover Road, Plymouth PL6 7PY, United Kingdom

Distributed by National Book Network

British Library Cataloguing in Publication Information Available

Library of Congress Cataloging-in-Publication Data

Darnall, Douglas.
   Beyond divorce casualties : reunifying the alienated family / Douglas Darnall.
     p. cm.
   Includes bibliographical references and index.
   ISBN 978-1-58979-415-3 (pbk. : alk. paper)
   1. Parental alienation syndrome—Prevention. 2. Children of divorced parents—Family relationships. 3. Custody of children—Psychological aspects. I. Title.
RJ506.P27D367 2010
618.92'89—dc22

                                                                    2009047683

∞™ The paper used in this publication meets the minimum requirements of American National Standard for Information Sciences—Permanence of Paper for Printed Library Materials, ANSI/NISO Z39.48-1992.

Printed in the United States of America

To my parents, Paul and Jan Tanner,
for sharing their wisdom and experiences.
Their love and support has been invaluable.

Contents

Acknowledgments

The success of *Divorce Casualties* over the past ten years has grown beyond my expectations. Every day I receive e-mails from frightened and angry parents feeling helpless against the perils of high-conflict divorce and alienation. Parents are seeking answers and support from someone who understands what they are going through. They look to the Internet for answers, anything that will give them direction to regain some control from the damage caused by alienation. *Divorce Casualties* has struck a nerve with these parents struggling to keep their loving relationship with their children alive.

The success of *Divorce Casualties* has prompted a need to go the next step, *Beyond Divorce Casualties,* because much has since been learned about alienation. There is new hope for reunification with new treatment protocols being developed. The arguments about the validity or mere existence of parental alienation and parental alienation syndrome are being successfully challenged, though in some camps the arguments have not been totally abated. After ten years, alienation has become more pervasive.

William Bernet, M.D., has compiled in his book a summary of extensive research supporting the inclusion of the concept of parental alienation in the new DSM-V (Bernet, 2010). The research has been presented to the DSM-V Task Force, the component of the American Psychiatric Association that will decide which mental conditions should be included in DSM-V. Bernet argues that parental alienation could be considered a "mental disorder," in which case it would be called *parental alienation disorder.* However, he says parental alienation could also be considered a "relational problem," in which case it would be called *parental alienation relational problem* in DSM-V. If Bernet is successful, it will quiet many of the opponents and legal pundits calling parental alienation "junk science."

Deciding what to include in the revised edition of *Divorce Casualties* was an enormous task because of the wealth of information published in the past ten years. The draft of the revision was over 700 pages—too long for a book of this nature. It was decided to divide the draft into two books;

the first book is *Divorce Casualties: Understanding Parental Alienation* and the second book is *Beyond Divorce Casualties: Reunifying the Alienated Family*, a book introducing parents to an intervention model. The two books work together. *Beyond Divorce Casualties: Reunifying the Alienated Family* is possible because of the efforts of committed mental health and legal professionals, authors, and researchers who have contributed to our knowledge about how to work with these families. I cannot say enough about how grateful I am for all the families that have shared their stories and experiences and unknowingly contributed to this book. The vast number of stories could be a book in itself.

Many of my dearest friends have helped with editing and offering suggestions about the contents of the book. I cannot say enough about how grateful I feel. I wish to thank Barbara Steinberg, Ph.D., for her contribution to the spontaneous reunification chapter; and Amy Baker, Ph.D. for her analysis about the underlying theory of the book. She was very helpful, challenging some of the premises in the book. Terry Heltzel, Ph.D.; Albert Linder, L.I.S.W.; Mary Wargo; Brianna Darnall, M.S.; Michele Hawn, M.P.C.C.; and Bill Alley, M.S.W., have all contributed their wisdom and their professional insight and experiences. Deirdre Petrich, Ph.D., L.P.C.C., offered a unique perspective with her contribution about pets and custody. Collette and David Summers's passion for the book was inspirational and motivating. They shared their life experiences, and insight about the perils of parental alienation and parental alienation syndrome. Not the least, my agents and friends, Denise Marcil and Anne Marie O'Farrell, have inspired me with their confidence in what I set out to accomplish.

Jan, my wife, has sacrificed our time together while I worked and researched material for this book. She helped with editing and gave her clinical impressions about the book's contents. My daughters, Brianna, a law student at Duquesne University Law School, and Lindsey, a research technologist at Cleveland Clinic Foundation, are great and are always a source of support. I love them all for standing beside me.

Preface

Beyond Divorce Casualties: Reunifying the Alienated Family is intended to educate you about the symptoms of parental alienation and how to prevent the more severe consequences of parental alienation syndrome. *Divorce Casualties* may have left you hanging, wanting more information about what to do with the severely alienated child and the alienating parent. *Beyond Divorce Casualties* continues where *Divorce Casualties* left off, offering greater detail about how to intervene. *Beyond Divorce Casualties* is a workbook, requiring you to rethink how to intervene with the other parent and your children. There are many real-life examples of alienating behavior plus exercises and specific instructions for how to change your feelings and behavior. The book's underlying assumption is the belief that you have power to change even if you have no power to change the other parent. By changing your behavior and attitude, you are likely to see a difference in how the other parent behaves toward you. These changes will in turn influence your children's behavior.

I have the same problem in this book as I did writing *Divorce Casualties*. Families today are different from years past. Some of you are parents who are divorced or anticipating divorce and are struggling with the relationship with your ex-spouse. Other readers are parents who were never married. Gay parents have become an issue. There are grandparents raising grandchildren, single mothers with children from more than one father, blended families with two sets of stepchildren, teenagers raising babies, and more recently donor babies. Although I do not mean to exclude any of my readers, I have decided to take the easy way out by writing this book as if my readers were two divorced parents. Thus, "ex-spouse" is used for parents who were never married as well as for those who were. I have also tried to stay gender neutral because an alienating parent can be a mother, a father, a significant other, and even a grandparent. The debate that only fathers are victims and mothers are alienators is false. In fact, there are many contentious divorces where both parents are actively alienated.

Writing *Beyond Divorce Casualties* required my looking at parental alienation and parental alienation syndrome from both the alienating parent's and targeted parent's perspective.

Whatever your circumstances, you will learn the following:

- What reunification therapy is and how it works.
- How to prepare for reunification.
- How to effectively work with your attorney, mediators, parent coordinators, court appointed evaluators, and counselors.
- How to identify and overcome obstacles to reunification.
- Methods for repairing a damaged relationship with your children.
- Learning a model for change.
- Preparing and responding to a spontaneous reunification.
- How to say "good-bye."

While reading the book, you may sometimes feel overwhelmed, thinking, "I can't do this." This is a common reaction but you must remember that alienation did not occur overnight. You may have not seen it coming but the underpinnings for alienation have probably been going on for months if not years. It took time for alienation to take a hold on your children; it will take equal if not more time to repair the damage, especially if you don't have the court's support to somehow restrain the alienating parent's behavior.

You will learn from reading this book to look closely at your own behavior and be more aware of how your children are affected by the nuances of what you say and do. At first, learning to be more sensitive about alienation may stifle your spontaneity. However, once you become accustomed to thinking differently, you will be more careful about what you say to your children and monitor your behavior accordingly. Like any new learning, this becomes easier with time.

Learning new behavior is not easy. It begins by understanding what it is you want to accomplish and then learning the tools for change. Reading a book about change does not replace the value of therapy. That is not the purpose of this book. The struggle you may experience reading this book is learning about change and the intense work needed on your part to make change happen. You could be reading this book with the attitude that you have done nothing wrong, and that may be true, but you are part of the solution for repairing the bridge between you, your children, and yes, your ex-spouse. The question you have to ask yourself is how hard are you willing to work?

This book will give you many tools for change. Some tools will make sense and others not. You will decide what works for you. Since publishing the original *Divorce Casualties*, there have been hundreds of peer-reviewed journal articles written about parental alienation and parental alienation syndrome. I cannot address all that is written about parental alienation and parental alienation syndrome in the limited space provided here. I have not referenced many excellent articles and studies in this book because of limited space. I was not able to describe the infinite number of case studies that have come to my attention for the same reason. There just isn't enough space in this book to say all that can be said about alienation. True, the debate about alienation continues but that is the nature of science, to question and argue. The fact that the debate has continued for more than twenty years should say to the skeptics that something very real is happening to these families. We all can't be delusional or misguided. Something must be addressed for the sake of the children's welfare for years to come. Whatever the arguments, the children are the victims. We, the mental health professionals, the courts, and parents have the responsibility to the children who are the helpless victims, to stop the fighting and get on with repairing damaged families.

I have tried to write in a manner that would prevent the reader from feeling defensive. Do not feel discouraged if you are not the perfect parent. No one can make that claim. All you can do is aspire to be a better parent. Perhaps you will learn that much of what you have been doing is right, although there is more you can do to reduce alienation. Parenting is a full-time job that takes a conscious effort on your part. Most of the parents I have worked with do more right than wrong, and I am sure this is true of you, too. While reading the book you have an opportunity to complete exercises designed to stimulate your thinking and help enhance your awareness about your parenting during this trying time. I have used real-life examples to help you understand the issues more clearly and apply them to your own family.

All parents reading this book want the same opportunities: to share in raising their children in peace, to give them the love and protection they deserve, and to revel in their future successes. I sincerely wish you and your children all the best toward accomplishing this goal.

1

A New Beginning

Parental alienation (PA) and parental alienation syndrome (PAS) have been talked about and bantered about for the past fifteen years. I continue receiving e-mails from parents feeling victimized by alienation after learning there was a name for what they are experiencing with their children and ex-spouse. Parents are learning, usually after a web search, about PA and PAS. They are looking for support and answers. Many parents express relief that they are not alone with their peril. Some parents expressed relief, knowing that they were not crazy. They frequently ended their e-mail asking "What can I do about it?" and hoping for a simple answer. Sadly, there is no simple answer. All I am able to do is to offer hope and encouragement to not give up.

> *"I showered the court with everything I had about PAS; the judge laughed at me."*

Not much has changed in the past fifteen years. Alienation is alive and well. The results from an unpublished study of parents who completed the Parental Alienation Inventory (Darnall 1993, see appendix A) found a majority of parents involved in high-conflict litigation expressed the wish that the other parent would "just disappear." If you are the rejected or targeted parent, you have a good reason to be cynical. Try not to be discouraged if the other parent refuses to work with you.

The response to the first edition of *Divorce Casualties: Protecting Your Children from Parental Alienation* (1998) was very heartening. Thousands of parents have read the first edition and still clamored for more information. The revised *Divorce Casualties: Understanding Parental Alienation* (2008) provides greater clarity about PA and PAS, describing the more common symptoms of each (I hesitate to use the word "symptom" because of the controversy). Also discussed are approaches for differentiating between true and false allegations, explanations for what motivates a parent to alienate, advice on what action to take when responding to various

1

alienating tactics, and arguments refuting the controversy around the validity of PA and PAS. What is not addressed in detail is the question most often asked, "What do I do about it?" This book, *Beyond Divorce Casualties*, discusses how to motivate the unmotivated, methods for changing irrational beliefs, overcoming obstacles to a healthy parent/child relationship, and reunification therapy with the severely alienated child.

The answer for what to do begins by understanding PA and PAS. This is not as simple as knowing the definition of the terms because what you are observing or experiencing can also be due to estrangement, behaviors that have nothing to do with alienation but instead cause serious parent-child problems. Common examples of estrangement are a parent's failure to bond with the children, punitive parenting, neglect, mental illness, substance abuse, personality disorders, and physical or sexual abuse. Because of the parent's emotional investment in the case, he or she may be too close to see how they contribute to the parent-child problem. For this reason, an expert on PA, family systems theory, child development, or family therapy needs to complete a thorough evaluation of all parties involved in the litigation before beginning reunification. One point that must be emphatically understood is that a child's anger or resistance toward a parent because of physical or sexual abuse *is not* PAS.

"My son has said he wants to get his dad's gun and kill me and they pray for me to go to hell."

Josie's Story

"I recognize now that I have been both an alienator and increasingly the alienated parent. The reason that I am researching this now is that telling my son's father and my son that I could no longer live as a family in one house triggered a very troublesome change in both of their behavior toward me. The son I was close to is now distant and argumentative and extremely protective of his father, to the point of being his emotional caretaker as the expense of his own life. I realize that I needed help for myself and for my son and have begun to take the steps to get it. I realize now that what I am facing is far more complex than how co-dependence and domestic violence affect me and my son and that I need to seek professional help for multiple psychological issues.

"I am writing because your article helped me realize my own role in what is happening and my responsibility to change the situation and how I see my position as a "pre-divorce" situation, complicated by a long history of spousal abuse and threats by a man who is physically disabled and psychologically challenged by bipolar disorder. My story feels more complicated than a divorce situation because of these issues. I have spent several years taking care of my son's father financially and supporting him emotionally while essentially living as roommates (not spouses) since our son was born. During my pregnancy, I was physically abused and have since been suffering from psychological abuse and threats (twelve years). This has taken a toll on my personality and physical health and the stress has become unmanageable for me.

"As my son is growing up I see that he is showing signs of social alienation as he identifies with his father. My decision to change the situation and live separately and closer to my family and friends was to get back my self-respect and give my son the experience of being with people who show their love for each other in healthy ways. Since telling them both that I intended to make the change, they have become much closer in some very unhealthy ways and their reaction convinced me to try again to be a family.

"Four weeks and a move across the country later my son appears to be afraid to spend time with me, to show me affection and is argumentative and aggressive and unwilling to listen to anything I am saying about his father's irrational behaviors and accusations against me. In the past, I believed I was comforting my son by explaining that his father was not a bad person but was ill and that he deserved compassion but that he was wrong to be acting aggressively and it was my job to protect us. I thought I was doing the right thing. This is what I am trying to come to terms with and what your article has helped me to understand in a more rational way than I could have before. I was an unconscious/passive alienator. Part of the abuse against me was for his father to threaten me that he would prevail with authorities at being an aggressive alienator. I took steps to remove myself and my son from the abusive family situation by living separately but close to his father. That is causing his father to be an unconscious alienator, motivated by irrational fears that he is going to live under a bridge and never see his son. His father is now calling me mentally ill in front of our son and spending hours with him behind closed doors where he is aggressively told I am not welcome.

"My son is showing me affection in short isolated moments but never in the same room as his father. Now I find myself being aggressive

3

toward his father for abusing me psychologically and for manipulating our son. As he calls me a fat pig; I call him a poor excuse of a man. You get the picture. Talk about a reciprocal psychosocial dynamic, this is really it and it is truly a horrible experience. I know I am in a dangerous situation. I am living in fear and isolation in my own home on a completely new level. I'm getting help for myself and for my son and will do what I can do to protect our son from the harm that parental alienation will cause him; I need to find a way to navigate the fine line between child protection, self protection, and being the alienator.

"I have very little hope that his father will do the same. As much as I hate to admit it, it is my expectation that he will lash out at me and be openly hateful and manipulative toward our son even more so than he is now. I'm afraid my son's life and mine are going to be ruined and I'm so ashamed. Even now, my son tells me that he and his dad have talked it over and now he won't leave his dad home alone and come with me (to see one of his favorite people). He is taking care of his father emotionally because father goes into deep depression. Instead of being encouraged to go into the world to engage in other meaningful relationships he stays by his father's side. I find this unbearable and I'm desperate to allow my son to experience a healthier lifestyle.

Josie's story demonstrates that alienation is just one of many issues that parents and children alike are exposed to during the breakdown of the family. Josie has the insight to recognize how she was both a victim and a perpetrator of alienation. She recognizes how mental illness, a child's enmeshment with an ill parent, and allegations of abuse added to the complexity of issues that she and her family faced. Multiple issues are more the norm than the exception for high-conflict families. Many parents involved in high-conflict litigation are quick to blame alienation for their problems with their children, but this isn't always the case, as Josie recognizes.

How do you know if you are a target of alienation? You must begin by knowing there are two scenarios of alienation for consideration: the alienating parent's behavior and your child's response to the alienation. Adding to the confusion is the role of estrangement for explaining parent/child conflicts. You must understand what the terms mean before drawing any conclusions about being targeted. How to intervene in a high-conflict divorce where there are allegations about alienation is not simple. Interventions may be different, depending on the degree, severity, and duration of the alienation. This is true for both the alienating parent and the alienated child.

Parental Alienation

Parents can be too quick to accuse the other parent of alienating their child without first understanding what is meant by parental alienation. The parent may see unexplained changes in their child's behavior, believing that the changes are caused by the other parent's desire to vilify the targeted parent. The accusations can be completely out of line.

There is not always agreement on the meaning of *parental alienation*. The terms parental alienation and parental alienation syndrome are sometimes used interchangeably because of the controversy about the word "syndrome" (Darnall 2008). This only adds to the confusion about how to identify and treat alienation. The terms describe two very different patterns of behavior.

The definition below is a revised definition that identifies the more common elements of alienation from an unpublished study (Darnall 1993). A factor analysis of 199 participants involved in contentious custody litigation and who completed the Parental Alienation Inventory (Darnall 1998) identifies a cluster of behaviors and beliefs that can be attributed to alienating parents:

- Resistance or refusal to comply with court orders.
- Critical of the targeted parent's parenting skills.
- Denigration of the targeted parent to the child.
- A belief that all would be better off if the targeted parent would disappear.
- Contentious litigation.
- Unrelenting anger.

The revised definition describes the alienating parent's behavior and not the child's behavior. You must keep this in mind when trying to understand the differences between PA and PAS. A comprehensive definition that allows for the nuances of alienation is: A parent's purposeful campaign of vilification characterized by anger, resistant and inconsistent compliance with court orders, conscious or unconscious denigration of the child's other parent, and interference with the other parent/child relationship.

Parents, grandparents, stepparents, significant others, and even interested professionals can alienate. Imagine for a moment what it feels like for the child in the following situation:

- To hear a parent say, "Well, you'll be living with scum now but never mind, we'll get you back here."
- Jerry's mother told him to call his father "Jeff" rather than Dad and to call his new stepfather Dad instead of Larry.
- A father fearing he would lose custody after the mother and her new husband moved some distance away, said to his daughter, "You will never see me again if your mother moves."

As preposterous as these statements sound, they were said by alienating parents. These parents may have known better than to make such statements, but obsessed parents rationalize and feel justified making these types of statements. For the obsessed parent, eliminating the other parent from the child's life is a bigger concern than considering the child's feelings or the child's long-term best interest.

Alienation has many subtleties that you may not have considered. Examples that you may have not considered are:

- Preventing a scheduled exchange or visit contrary to court orders.
- Scheduling activities that compete with the other parent's parenting time.
- Scheduling your child with an excessive number of activities that interfere with parenting time.
- Making denigrating comments to the child about the targeted parent.
- Criticizing or making demands to the other parent about their parenting skills.
- Having secrets with your child from the other parent.
- Initiating frequent trips to court intending to restrict or eliminate parenting time.
- Secret rendezvous.
- Giving the child unjustified reasons to fear the targeted parent.
- Refusing the targeted parent access to medical and school records.

- Hindering the parent's access to the child's schedule of social activities.

Examples of alienating techniques are infinite. What is common to all the techniques is the conscious or unconscious intent by the alienating parent to strengthen their relationship with their child at the expense of the other parent. Disrupting the progression of the alienation depends in part on the parent's attitude, belief systems, psychological makeup, and motivation. You will learn there are clear distinctions between the naive, active, and obsessed parent. These distinctions are important because the intervention for slowing or eliminating alienation is different.

Naive Alienation

Naive alienators recognize the value of the children's relationship with the other parent prior to and after the separation or divorce. They sincerely strive to keep the relationship strong but occasionally do or say something that inadvertently suggests there is something amiss with the targeted parent. The child may hear a parent say:

- "Your father isn't paying the medical bills."
- "We can only afford to go out to eat after I receive the child support. If it's late, we have to eat at home."
- "You have a temper like your mother."
- "Your father is not helpless. He can get his own schedule of your soccer games."

Children, even in a tightly knit family, will occasionally hear derogatory comments said about the other parent. They learn to let the comments go without much of a reaction. Naive parents learn from their mistakes and usually think about how their behavior may impact on the children and then make any necessary apologies and move on. They rarely need therapy and their court appearances are few.

Active Alienation

Parents who *actively alienate*, after some reflection, usually know better than to alienate. These parents struggle with unresolved issues that trigger intense emotional reactions. Reminders of the reasons for the divorce, the adversarial nature of the court proceedings, and hearing from the attorney about the court date are all common triggers. During the course of the divorce, there are frequently long lapses of time when nothing is happening with the case. Both parents find some comfort during these lapses until that inevitable phone call from the attorney. Hearing the attorney's voice provokes the anxiety and takes them out of the fog that comes with denial and adjustment.

A common trigger for an active alienator is the introduction of the other parent's new significant other to the children. The new significant other may be a reminder of the rejection or betrayal felt by a rejected spouse. He or she may fear losing or competing with the new significant other for the children's affections or loyalty or may relive the finality of the end of what was once a loving relationship. The triggers cause an emotional swell thereby rendering the parent a temporary loss of self-control and good judgment. After regaining control, the parent may feel upon reflection remorseful for how he or she behaved and worried about how their child felt after witnessing the meltdown. To lessen guilt, the parent may blame the other parent for what they feel or make excuses to minimize the children's feelings. The targeted parent may not always know about the alienating behavior unless told by the children. Children may hear a parent say:

- "Jim called me a bitch in front of the kids."
- "Bob told the kids that I couldn't take them to the movies because they are afraid of me."
- "I don't care what your father says. He can care less about your feelings."
- "I am not going to let Stacy spend the night with you. You don't know the first thing about taking care of a three-year-old."

You can hear the anger in these parents' voices. The parent's anger interferes with working with the other parent. The failure to control anger is common for the active alienator. After they calm down, they usually see the error of their ways. They may rationalize their anger as justified, and perhaps that is true. The problem for these parents is their inability to maintain self-control when triggered. They know better than to dump their anger on the children but they will say "I know it's wrong but can't help it." The difference between the active and the obsessed parent is the obsessed parent's failure to admit any wrong doing, and their inability to heal or take any responsibility for their behavior. Active parents may require individual therapy to help put these issues to rest and allow them to move on.

Obsessed Alienation

The distinction between how an active alienator and the obsessed parent behaves is the obsessed parent's persistence, an inability to empathize with either the children or the targeted parent, the inability to forgive, an insatiable need to be in control, and inability to see any viewpoint but their own. No one is going to tell these parents they are wrong or that there is another point of view. They do not see the harm they are causing their children, instead professing to protect the children. No one, including the court, is going to say he or she is wrong. Their goal is to remove the children from the targeted parent's life. These parents use many tactics similar to brainwashing. They attempt to psychologically and physically isolate the children from the targeted parent and their significant others, barrage the children with distorted reality or delusional beliefs, and denigrate the targeted parent with falsehoods. I concur with the argument that the obsessed parent's persistent attempt to alienate is child abuse.

The most severe example is false allegations of physical or sexual abuse. What these parents fail to realize is the emotional and social consequences to the child if the parent succeeds with their allegations. The child will go through life being a victim of a falsehood and likely lose forever what the targeted parent could have given to his or her son or daughter and future grandchildren. There is also the risk that the accused could spend years in prison. West Virginia (2008) is the first state to criminalize false allegations of abuse during the custody litigation. The sanction can be a fine up to a thousand dollars and/or two hundred hours of community service. All states should follow West Virginia's lead.

Obsessed parents can use very creative tactics to alienate. Most pronounced are the relentless anger and fervor to eliminate the other parent from the children's lives. Frequently you can hear the obsessed parent's motivation in their statements to the attorney and counselors:

- "Mary Beth grabs Larry's face and tells him he better not grow up to be like his dad."
- "I don't care what the court says. She has good reason to fear her father."
- "I know you cannot tell me you are afraid of your father."
- "I will never give up trying to get you to live with me."
- "No court is going to tell me what to do. They can send me to jail."
- "Robbie will understand that I am only trying to protect him from his mother."

- "You can see it in his eyes. It is only a matter of time—he will sexually abuse my daughter."

- "I know my daughter is afraid of her mother and won't admit to anyone that her boyfriend sexually abused her. I don't care what the so-called experts say, she is not going over to her mother's house until the boyfriend is in jail."

Obsessed parents will not listen to anyone who refuses to share in their crusade. They are angry, unwavering, unrelenting, and aggressive in their assertions. They will fire attorneys and counselors that waver or refuse to be advocates. They are not motivated to seek professional help unless it suits their needs. Contrary to what is professed, the child's needs are irrelevant unless the obsessed parent believes the counselor will side with the obsessed parent and become a crusader.

Obsessed alienators have a fervent cause: to destroy the targeted parent. They rationalize their behavior believing they or the children are victims of imagined abuse or betrayal. Personality disorders or mental illness can contribute to the obsessed parent's irrational thinking. Rarely does the obsessed alienator have enough self-control or insight to contain their rage when confronted with the prospect of having to interact with the targeted parent. Sadly, the children are the target of the rage by exposing them to their alienating manipulations. Reasoning rarely works with these parents because any questioning or challenge is taken as an attack. Feeling defensive, the obsessed becomes more entrenched in the delusion.

Parental Alienation Syndrome

Gardner (1998) defined PAS as "a disturbance in which children are preoccupied with deprecation and criticism of a parent—denigration that is unjustified and/or exaggerated." This is the distinction between parental alienation and parental alienation syndrome. I don't want to harp on this distinction, but I have to because not making the distinction is confusing and hinders treatment.

"She makes up excuses why they cannot come for a visit. They are now to the point where they come up with reasons on their own."

Gardner's "eight cardinal symptoms of parental alienation syndrome" focus on the child and not the parent's behavior. The behaviors include:

- **Persistent campaign of denigration:** The campaign of denigration is heard when the child is relentless in name calling, criticizing, and defacing the targeted parent. No amount of convincing can change the child's attitude or language. They are true believers.

- **Weak, frivolous, and absurd rationalizations for the deprecation:** The child will offer absurd excuses to hate, such as, "He made me eat my peas. I have to go to bed by nine o'clock. He looks at me strange."

- **Lack of ambivalence:** The targeted parent is all-bad with no redeeming qualities. A common example is showing the child vacation photographs in which they are smiling with the targeted parent. When asked about the smile, the child will say, "I am faking it."

- **The independent thinker phenomena:** Some children understand accusations of alienation though they may not understand the terms. The alienating parent will put ideas in the child's mind or he or she hears arguments that denigrate the targeted parent. Over time after hearing a barrage, the child will integrate the parent's beliefs into his or her own. After all, the child does not want to believe that the parent raising him or her would lie. The targeted parent has very little defense against the torrent of accusations. Perceptive children will sense something is wrong and learn the alienating word. The child will insist that his or her feelings are his or her own, independent of the alienating parent. It is reasonable to suspect alienation when a child proclaims their independent thinking without being asked. The alienated child will jump at the chance to take the alienating parent's side or defend the alienating parent regardless of how absurd the allegations may sound to the interested listener. Whatever the alienating parent says is true and the targeted parent is a liar.

- **Absence of guilt over cruelty to and/or exploitation of the alienated parent:** The alienating child typically knows that his behavior and comments toward the targeted parent are hurtful. They do not care. They express no empathy, remorse, or guilt because they believe they are justified to feel the way they do. To an outside observer, the child appears to gloat about their hatred toward the parent.

- **Presence of borrowed scenarios:** The hateful child may justify his or her feelings from scenarios offered by the alienating parent. This is not always done deliberately but it can happen with devastating consequences, particularly if the allegations involve physical or sexual abuse. An alienated child may rationalize his hatred by saying he remembers his father abusing his mother when he was two years old. Two-year-olds will have no such memories. The rationalization comes from what is overheard from adults or was told by someone directly, believing that the allegation must be true. Borrowed scenarios become especially dangerous when there are false allegations of sexual abuse.

- The animosity spreads to the extended family of the alienated parent. With no justification, personal experience, and without reason, the child expresses hate and anger toward the targeted parent, significant others, or extended family.

You will notice that Gardner's symptoms focus on the child and not the parent's behavior. The child's behaviors are a manifestation of an alienating adult, sometimes even from a sibling's behavior. Adding to the confusion is the occasional child who appears alienated but has learned to play the role to contain his histrionic parent. The child chooses to keep peace by playing the role rather than facing the parent's wrath. The child is a victim of emotional blackmail. The qualified evaluator has the task of learning the truth.

Estrangement

Estrangement must be considered as a possible explanation of an impaired parent-child relationship. Kelly and Johnson (2001) defined estrangement "as a child having a rational reason to reject a parent because of neglect, physical or sexual abuse, abandonment or domestic violence." For our purposes, a broader definition of estrangement may better help differentiate between problematic parent behavior and alienation. Simply put, estrangement is any parent-child problematic behavior, excluding alienation. Most often, the cause of a child's rejection or parent-child conflicts is a combination of a parent's alienating behavior and the targeted parent's estrangement. On many occasions the targeted parent will unwittingly contribute to the parent/child problems. This is understandable because the targeted parent will get defensive and feel threatened by the alienating parent's behavior.

Minimizing the Damage

While working toward reunification or repairing a damaged relationship caused by parental alienation, you must also consider how to behave to prevent further damage. You must face some realities. The other parent may have no or little concern for how you feel. Arguing about fairness will get you nowhere. Expect the other parent to put their self-interest before yours. Do not be surprised to be the target of blame and irrational allegations. Your frustration is understandable because you know that you are powerless to change the alienating parent's behavior. It is understandable that at times you are angry and depressed. What you do have control over is how you respond to the alienating parent and, more importantly, to your child.

Reunification is a process of repairing damaged relationships. Concurrent with the process has to be your awareness about what you shouldn't do because these things would further damage the relationship between you, your child, and, yes, the other parent.

While working on reunification, you must concentrate on two tasks. The first is not to retaliate with your own alienating behavior, and the second is to build or keep strong your relationship with your child. By now you should have a good understanding about what is alienating behavior. If you have in the past alienated because you were naive, there should be no problem with your stopping the behavior. If you know, after some reflection, that you have alienated because you lost control of your behavior and you accept responsibility for your wrong doing, then you have a lot to gain by reading on. Your goal needs to be learning more self-control and focusing on strengthening your relationship with your child and reducing your alienating behavior. You need to spend loving time with your child, make up after arguments or punishment, let your child know he or she is prized, and not blame your child for what the other parent is doing. The majority of your time spent with your children should be positive.

If not, you have work to do. You need to make a conscious effort to do what you already know puts a smile on your child's face. That is how you know that what you are doing is working. Parents ask, "How do I know if what I am doing is right?" The answer is in the child's behavior and the look on their face. Another way of answering the question is making a decision that will reduce your child's anxiety. Children do not want to fear you; otherwise, they will be drawn toward the parent who makes them most comfortable. Can you guess who that is?

The Alienating Cycle

Some parents are predisposed to alienate because of their maladaptive personality traits, their inability to heal from feeling betrayed, and adherence to irrational beliefs. It is not always easy to guess if your spouse, soon to be ex-spouse, will alienate but keep in mind that alienation can begin well before the separation while a parent is trying to position himself or herself for custody. There are some signs of risk to look for but do not fall into the trap of making assumptions or diagnoses. Many parents accuse their ex-spouse of having a borderline or narcissistic personality disorder. The parent may be correct but making the diagnosis or accusing a parent of being obsessed or of having a personality disorder is wrong and damaging. Some of the cues to look for, suggesting a risk for alienation, include the following:

- Persistent anger without an ability to recover or heal.
- Adhering to irrational beliefs when the parent is not able to recognize alternative explanations for what is occurring; comments like "I don't want to hear what you say," "You just will lie anyway," and "What does a man know about raising children?"
- When there appears to be an unhealthy bond with the child and one parent tries to exclude the other parent or actively minimizes participation from even the most basic parenting responsibilities; complaints like "I will do it; you don't know the first thing about how to care for your son."
- Frequent fights where the parents never resolve any issues but instead walk away in frustration; comments like "There is no use talking to you."
- A history of false allegations of abuse from either the child or the spouse; comments like "I know it is only a matter of time being you will abuse my child like you abused me."
- A parent's barrage of blame with no ability to accept any responsibility for what is ailing the family.

- Threats to abduct the children; comments like "You will never see your children again" and "I will go where you will never find us."

When you recognize any of the risk factors, it is not always easy to know what to do. There is no simple, one-answer-fits-all. Some necessary steps to reduce the risk of successful alienation include these practices:

- Control your reaction to accusations. Take time to think about how you are going to respond. For the time being, you may have to walk away, especially if the children are within earshot.

- Focus on keeping your relationship with the children strong by spending positive time with them—be a source of positive praise and reinforcement, learn to mentor, and never leave them with the other parent without first making up after an argument or punishment.

- Avoid your own alienating behavior. Do not retaliate against your spouse, especially in your child's presence.

- Do not violate court orders, causing your attorney to defend your behavior rather than taking the offensive.

A Word about Revenge

I don't know if the parent reading this book feels he or she is the target of alienation or is the parent obsessed in the desire to eliminate the other parent from the children's lives. Either way, it is easy to feel angry and betrayed, leaving you with a desire for revenge.

You may believe you have good reason for feeling the way you do. Regardless, your desire for revenge is a rope around your soul that will smother any hope to heal. You may learn different methods for coping with alienation and improving your relationship with your children, but if you continue to hang on to your desire for revenge, your efforts in the long term will fail. You will find no lasting resolutions to your problems.

Also, keep in mind that alienation can backfire. Many children who were once alienated from a parent later learn what happened and then redirect their anger and hate toward the alienating parent. Don't think this cannot happen to you. You have to get past your hate and desire for revenge. Holding on to your hate only hurts you and your children. Don't think your children won't someday notice.

Jerry's Story

Jerry wanted counseling because he didn't think he could any longer control his rage against his alienating mother. He cried and his hands quivered when describing his anger. Now twenty-eight years old, Jerry was able to look back and see how he was brainwashed into believing he had reasons to hate his father.

Jerry, like many young adults, was curious to meet his father after many years of separation. He learned that his father was nothing like his mother described. He was kind and sympathetic. Shortly after re-uniting with his father, his father suddenly died, leaving Jerry enraged because of the time lost with his father. He didn't know what to do with his anger and grief, other than to direct his rage toward his mother. He felt betrayed by his mother for the years of her lies. Jerry wanted nothing to do with his mother. Now his mother was paying the price for her alienation.

The Alienating Cycle

The alienating cycle can begin prior to the separation, when one parent is trying to jockey him- or herself into a stronger position for the child's loyalty at the other parent's expense. Do not confuse the parent's anger toward you with alienation. A parent can get angry without alienating. For alienation to occur, your child has to be exposed, either directly or indirectly, to alienating tactics that bring the child into the fray, risking damage to the other parent/child relationship. Whether the child is dragged into the alienation depends on the parent's persistence and the intensity of the alienating behavior, the child's ability to resist manipulations, and how the other parent responds to the child. The targeted parent can make matters worse if he or she reacts with his or her own alienating behavior.

Everyone gets angry, especially during litigation. You cannot assume that an angry parent is an alienating parent. There are many things that can incite alienation. The alienating process usually begins when a parent's emotions are aroused by something said or done by the other parent or even by a significant other. Circumstances, such as learning the risk of losing custody or restricted access to their children, can consume the parent with severe anxiety. Many judges will tell you that the introduction of a new boy- or girlfriend is a leading cause for why parents return to court. A new significant other can be very threatening to an insecure parent. Sometimes the significant other will feel threatened by the biological parent and begin alienating. Almost any event can start the progression. The alienating cycle has four phases: the triggers, the response, the counter-attack, and the respondent's response. It is helpful to understand the alienating progression because the model shows how both parents get caught up in the fray and how both have some responsibility for what happens to the children. The targeted parent may believe he or she is the victim and is helpless to stop the alienation, and to some extent that is true, but the targeted parent can make matters worse depending on how he or she responds to the child. This is particularly true if the child is showing signs of parental alienation syndrome.

Phase 1: Parent A Is Triggered and in Turn Triggers an Emotional Response in Parent B

You need to identify whether you are parent A or parent B to understand the examples in the alienating cycle. Parent A is the parent whose emotions are triggered and Parent B is the targeted parent.

When couples marry, they bring into the relationship a history of experiences, a way of seeing and interpreting their world, and beliefs about that world that influence their behavior. This composite of experience, perceptions, and beliefs is what defines their personality. It tells us something about how the individual is predisposed to react in their environment.

A trigger is any stimulus or activity that sets off an intense emotional reaction. The trigger may be something symbolic to the parent, totally irrational but nonetheless stirring strong emotional reactions. A trigger may not have anything to do with the divorce. The parent's personality or, in severe situations, the parent's pathology will influence how the parent responds. A trigger may be nothing more than an innocent comment that sets off an emotional tirade. In fact, sometimes one parent triggers the other parent without realizing what they have done to incite the reaction. A comment such as, "I don't even know what he is angry about" is common. The intense emotional reaction may leave the recipient parent confused. Triggers usually have symbolic significance so the reaction is out of proportion when compared to how most people would have reacted in a similar situation. This is what makes the behavior appear so irrational.

An action or comment from the ex-spouse can trigger an emotional reaction that sets off a maelstrom of hate and contempt and, possibly, alienation. Asking to change parenting time, buying your daughter a new bike, being late with your support check, returning your children thirty minutes late, or observing a change in your child's mood can all trigger alienation.

An example is a mother watching from inside the house while her ex-husband is picking up their son for his scheduled parenting time and seeing them excited to be together. The excitement arouses her emotions that may have nothing personally to do with either the father or son acting inappropriately. The father, in fact, may empathize with the mother if he understood what was happening behind closed curtains. To her, the son's excitement has become a symbol of betrayal and loss.

Exercise: What Are My Triggers?

The purpose of this exercise is to help you become more aware of comments or actions from others that trigger a strong emotional reaction. The exercise has two parts.

First, try remembering from your recent past comments or behaviors by your ex-spouse that triggered your anger or hurt. Do not censor yourself.

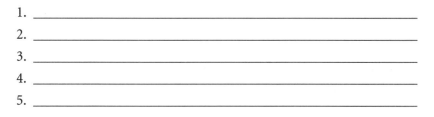

1. _____
2. _____
3. _____
4. _____
5. _____

Now, try to remember how you reacted or responded to the comments or behaviors.

1. _____
2. _____
3. _____
4. _____
5. _____

Try to answer honestly. Did your reaction help or hurt how you communicated with your ex-spouse? Did your child witness your behavior? How do you think your child felt witnessing your behavior? Do you need to learn better strategies for reacting when triggered?

Counseling Parent A requires the parent to accept responsibility for the emotional reaction and recognize that this is problematic behavior. The parent has to learn how to become desensitized to the triggers and change the irrational beliefs to more rational thinking.

Sometimes we can be surprised by what we can learn from others. A case in point is what I have learned from watching Cesar Millan's *The Dog Whisperer* on the National Geographic Channel. If you are not familiar with his television show, he is a specialist working with very violent and disobedient dogs. He works with the dog owners, teaching them how to take control of their dog to change its aggressive behavior. An important concept that he teaches the dog owners applies to all of us in our relationships with others, particularly an ex-spouse. What he says is that a dog will react to the owner's energy. If the owner is fearful or angry with the dog, the dog will react with fear or aggression. No words have to be spoken. The dog senses the owner's energy. So how does this apply to people? Have you ever reacted negatively to someone without their saying a word? Sometimes we find ourselves liking someone without a word being said. The other person can pick up on that energy and react accordingly. So how does this apply to two warring parents? Think about the kind of energy that radiates from you when you see your ex-spouse. Is it possible that your ex-spouse's hostility is a reaction to your energy, rather than to what you say? If you radiate hostility, you will get hostility in return. If you want to see a change in the relationship, any relationship, consciously try to change your energy from hostility to a more pleasant demeanor. It won't hurt you to be nice and respectful. Both you and your children will gain.

Phase 2: Parent B Becomes Defensive and Counter-attacks

When triggered, your immediate reaction may be to defend your behavior or retaliate. (Common sense should tell you to resist this impulse.) Alienators and even targeted parents are quick to defend their behavior because it is hard to admit that you may be wrong, especially to your ex-spouse who is ready to pounce on you. Parents in the heat of a divorce are sensitive and vulnerable to attack or anything they construe as criticism.

Like everyone else, you have an idea of how you want others to view you. If you are like most people, you want others to think of you as a good and loving parent, compassionate, honest, or all those things that you think you should be. This idealized image is like a facade around our true soul, how we really are but often do not want to admit. This wall is our armor, an insulator from the outside world. When someone speaks to you about "not letting anyone in" or "putting up a front," he or she is talking about your protective wall. If, either intentionally or by accident, someone threatens to penetrate this wall, your defenses immediately shore up the wall to minimize or avoid the hurt.

Exposing your vulnerabilities is the risk you take when you get close to someone you love. For this reason, trust in the relationship is important. You had to believe that the person you loved, went to bed with, and grieved, is now the very person who would not hurt you by using your vulnerabilities against you. Knowing this is no longer true may be the reason you feel betrayed. You will try to defend yourself, but your defenses will not always work.

Tip: Trust is the ability to predict. Are you predictable?

You need to learn to not react in a way that harms the relationship with the other parent, especially in front of your children. You can learn to express how you feel but do so with self-control. Do not make threats, call your ex-spouse names, or passively try to sabotage your children's relationship. Focus on the tone of your voice and the energy that radiates from you, both of which you have some control over.

Phase 3: Parent A Responds to the Counter-attack

The third phase of the alienating cycle is how you respond to any counter-attack. Your reactions may vary. Blaming, rationalizing, and denying are just some of the ways we defend ourselves from hurt. You may just rage. You may react without thinking but later make excuses for your behavior. You may retaliate with your anger, deny there is a problem, blame others, or force yourself to walk away from the conflict.

Tip: Do not respond to an attack with your own alienating behavior.

Whatever you do, this is a good place to stop the alienating cycle. It is one thing to get angry or tell your ex-spouse about your hurt, but it is quite another if you include your children in your response or react in a way that further harms the relationship between your ex-spouse and the children. The first scenario is two adults who have something to work out between themselves; the latter is alienation. So what is the difference?

Alienators focus on hurting the other parent's relationship with the children instead of preserving that relationship. Parents who are trying to preserve the relationship will consciously try to recognize the symptoms of alienation and behave in a way that prevents damage. As mentioned in chapter 1, this is not difficult for naive and active alienators but is extremely difficult for an obsessed parent who has rigid armor and a limited repertoire of responses.

Many times parents react quickly and later regret how they handled a situation. You are better able to prevent alienation if you make a commitment to yourself to stay calm, and regain your composure any time you feel triggered. You will be amazed how much this helps to prevent alienation and to preserve your own sense of integrity. Don't be afraid to excuse yourself, saying to the other parent that you want to calm down and not say anything hurtful.

If you are unable to control your behavior, consider getting therapy before causing further harm. Remember, the therapy is as much for your children as yourself. How you react to alienation is not always a simple matter of doing what you think is correct. It can involve a change in your attitude and a realization that you have to put your personal needs aside in deference to your children.

Tip: If you want to change how you feel, you must begin by changing your thinking and behavior.

Phase 4: Either Parent Uses that Response against Parent B

Either parent may react to the other parent with anger and retaliation. The targeted parent's counteroffensive rarely succeeds in getting the alienating parent to back off and consent to the parent's demands. If the alienating parent succumbs, it is not because they agree about something, but instead because they probably feel beaten down. In time, there will be another payback. The alienating parent will use the targeted parent's furious reaction against him or her, affirming to the children that their criticism against the targeted parent is justified. This reinforces the alienating parent's belief that they were right all along and their behavior was justified. For example, "I told you your father would have a fit if you asked him to stay home and go with us to the beach. He is not concerned about what you want. It's only about what he wants." What you have is chaos until everyone is, for the time being, beaten down until the next time.

Breaking the Cycle

Breaking the cycle does not completely depend on whether you are doing the alienating or are the targeted parent. In reality, you probably do some of both, even if you started out as the target. You can stop the alienating cycle by intervening at any point during the cycle and not behaving in a way that reinforces or is likely to perpetuate the other parent's alienating tactics. You may want to consider the following strategies to break the cycle.

- The best way not to reinforce the alienation is not to react to the alienating behavior. Regain your composure by walking away and saying we can talk later or taking some deep breaths and waiting for the pressure to leave your speech. If either you or your ex-spouse has pressured speech, there is a good chance that neither of you will listen nor hear what the other has to say.

- If you cannot communicate without losing control, use e-mail but remember your ex-spouse will save the e-mail for later use. Do not use vulgar language, make threats, or call names. There is a strong likelihood that your children will read the e-mail to reinforce the alienating parent's argument that you are an undeserving parent.

- Take time to think about how to respond. Do not allow yourself to feel pressured into a decision before you are ready. Remember, the more information you have prior to a decision, the better the decision. That also includes visualizing in your mind the consequences of your decision. *Visualizing* solutions rather than *thinking* is often more effective for many parents. It has been found that visualizing how you would like to respond increases the likelihood that you will later respond the way you rehearsed it in your mind. This is a very effective tool for learning new behavior.

- You may decide to negotiate a decision. Keep in mind a couple of points about negotiating. Negotiating begins with understanding that both of you have a different interest in the outcome of the negotiation. For your purpose, the common outcome should be to do no harm to your children and secondly to preserve the loving relationship between the children and both parents. Thinking otherwise means that one parent is only thinking about him- or herself and not the child. If you cannot ascribe to these beliefs, you may need professional help to see the flaws in your thinking. Secondly, recognize that to get or receive what you want you must be willing to give something in return. What are you willing to give in order to receive? To give nothing and expect everything is a violation of fairness and will raise the other parent's ire. Now begin the give and take (see box). In this example, the father had to give in order to get. This issue for the father is to be trustworthy and fair. He must do what he agrees to or he will violate his ex-spouse's trust and can forget about future cooperation.

- You may need to talk to a counselor or a mediator to help develop the skills so you can maintain calm, avoid triggers, and learn skills to negotiate. What you do not want to do is wait for the alienation to get worse. The purpose of seeing a counselor is to learn new skills, not because you are mentally ill. Remember, there is a point when severe alienation and parental alienation syndrome are extremely difficult to reverse.

In the first example, the parent reacts with alienating behavior:

"I have tickets to take Jimmy to the Indians' game. Can I bring him home late Sunday night?"

"No, you are always asking for more time. I am sick of your constantly asking for more time. I expect Jimmy home by six o'clock."

"You are being your usual bitch. I'll tell Jimmy that you refuse to let him go."

In this example, the parents avoid alienating behavior:

"I have tickets to take Jimmy to the Indians' game. Can I bring him home late Sunday night?"

"No, you are always asking for more time. I am sick of your constantly asking for more time. I expect Jimmy home by six o'clock."

"I know I have asked for more time in the past but this is an unusual opportunity to take Jimmy to the game. I know he would have fun and appreciate going. Can I make a suggestion? What can I give you that would make my having more time fair to you?"

"Why should I trust you?"

"You will only know by trying. I know you have asked that I buy Jimmy a winter jacket and boots. If I buy the jacket and boots in addition to my regular support, would you allow me to take Jimmy to the game?"

"I will try it but you better not let me down."

"I won't."

You can see from the two examples a different outcome if the requesting parent offers to give something in return for the other parent's support. There is no guarantee that giving in order to receive always works, but the alternative is guaranteed failure. You need to play the odds for improving the chance of success. If you anticipate resistance to your request, think beforehand about what you are willing to give in return for the other parent's cooperation.

3

Motivation for Change

You may be reading this chapter thinking about how to motivate the alienating parent or severely alienated child to change his or her behavior. All you know is rejection, anger, verbal attacks, and that cold and hostile attitude from your child. Parents have spent tens of thousands of dollars trying to reestablish a relationship with their child with no success. You may be one of these parents. By now, you know that threats, coercion, and court orders are not very effective for bringing about change. Motivating the unmotivated is not an easy task. For the obsessed parent, court orders are meaningless. We must accept some realities. It is easier to change ourselves than to change others. A caveat is the reality that changing our behavior may change how the other person responds to us. Circumstances apart from both parents can also motivate change.

There are no simple answers or protocols for bringing about change to a parent-child and parent-to-parent alienation. No single model will work for all circumstances. Bringing about lasting change will take more than what is offered in the following pages. We can learn about change from many different sources. Political science theory offers a model for change between political enemies. Therapists treating a drug addict will use an intervention to create an emotional crisis to motivate the unmotivated abuser into treatment. We can learn from these models and apply their principles to facilitate reunification. Throughout the rest of the book are different suggestions and exercises to help with your reunification. Some suggestions and exercises may not work, while other suggestions will help. You will not know what works until you make an honest effort to try rather than waiting for the other parent or child to change. *You* must take the initiative.

There is an infinite number of parents who have been estranged from their children because of alienation and who have frequented the courts with no or little success at breaking the stalemate. Courts have tried their best at breaking the stalemate but with limited success. The question is: How do you motivate the unmotivated parent to change? Court orders don't usually work with an obsessed parent. Family therapy has had very limited success. There is some hope with parent coordinators who have some degree of arbitration power to modify parenting time. You may have heard about reunification therapy but such therapy is in its infancy. Though we talk about reunification therapy later in the book, the treatment protocols are theoretical and not yet validated. Well-intended judges, mental health professionals, and attorneys are looking for answers.

Tip: There can be both intrinsic and extrinsic motivations for change.

There are no simple answers for promoting change. Solutions range from doing nothing and hoping the problem will go away to an involuntary change of custody to the alienated parent. The alienated parent frequently advocates that solution. The difficulty the court has before changing custody is deciding on balance what is best for the child: maintaining the status quo knowing that the child is making an adequate adjustment or taking a risk in changing custody and not knowing the consequences. Changing custody for most judges is very risky, especially with the severely alienated child who vehemently expresses a hatred or fear toward the rejected parent. The targeted parent must keep in mind that an alienating parent's refusal to foster a loving relationship with the rejected parent is only one of many criteria for deciding best interest. Other criteria can include the child's wishes, parent's mental health, and history of abuse. How much weight the judge puts on the different criteria is at his or her discretion. Not all states have specific written criteria for best interest. You need to talk with your attorney to learn your state's criteria for best interest.

Intrinsic Motivations for Change

A child's maturation (or a more mature way of thinking) can be a strong intrinsic motivator for change. The reframing of a child's irrational belief from "You are useless and deserve to be hated!" to "Can you help me with college?" often has a narcissistic or self-serving quality. Even hormonal changes and physical maturation can motivate reunification. One preteen daughter wanted a renewed relationship with her father because she was blossoming into womanhood and desired her father's affirmation. She wanted him to be involved in celebrating her emergence as a maturing female.

Motivating yourself and others to change is not simple. We can learn about motivating change from different sources One strategy for motivating change has been adapted from motivational interviewing (Miller and Rollnick 1991, Sobell and Sobell 2003). The model has four components that are applicable for both the alienating and targeted parent. The reason for considering both parents is that both parents usually have to make some changes with their beliefs and behavior. Whether you consider yourself a victim or are honest enough to admit your alienating behavior, the model may help you reconsider your thinking and your need to change.

Exercise: Reasons for Change

The first component of the motivational model is to list the reasons why it is in your and your child's best interests to change your thinking and behavior. List five reasons why change will better serve your children.

1. _____
2. _____
3. _____
4. _____
5. _____

List three personal risks to you and your child if your problem behaviors continue.

1. _____
2. _____
3. _____

What are your personal strengths and resources to promote change?

_____

_____

What are your ex-spouse's strengths and resources to promote change?

_____

_____

What problem-solving skills do you need to learn?

_____

_____

Where can you go to learn those skills?

_____

_____

Now take a moment and imagine what could be different if you followed through with what you have learned. How would your children benefit? Do you think your ex-spouse may react differently toward you if you made these changes?

Usually a therapist will help walk you through the steps for *why* you should change. This exercise is very difficult to do alone but hopefully the exercise will give you some insight about what to do better. You may consider writing a contract to remind yourself of the behaviors you want to change. Write the contract on a small piece of paper and carry it in your wallet or purse.

You and your children are better off if change can occur for intrinsic reasons because all of you will have more control over events. You will feel less victimized and avoid adverse consequences that can be painful. If you and your ex-spouse cannot come to an understanding and work together, then just wait until circumstances take over. You may not like what is forthcoming.

Personality Disorders

Parents with a severe personality disorder will have difficulty making changes without extensive therapy. What makes a person with a personality disorder so difficult is the belief that their maladaptive behavior in question is an asset and not something to change. These individuals vehemently defend and justify their behavior at all costs. They are quick to blame others for whatever problems occur. They do not see their contribution to the conflicts. These parents usually require professional treatment. Do not humiliate or degrade the other parent for choosing to get professional help. Do not use this as an excuse to call him or her "crazy" or "nuts," particularly to the children. Name calling is alienation and will cause the other parent to fight you all the way to court.

In recent years there has been a growing trend for angry parents to accuse the other parent of having a personality disorder. Angry parents may accuse the other parent of having a narcissistic or borderline personality disorder. This practice must stop. Parents are not qualified to make such a diagnosis. Doing so only hurts everyone involved and makes reunification more difficult. It is for this reason that the diagnostic criteria for personality disorders are not described in this book.

Extrinsic Motivation for Change

External events or situational changes in the child's life, such as a new significant other entering the parent's life, another divorce, a serious illness or death of a family member, a brush with the law, a traffic accident, loss of a scholarship, or no money for college, can motivate change. These changes can serve as a crisis that promotes change in a parent's or child's attitude. A crisis is a great motivation for change but timing is important. You must act while the crisis is occurring. Waiting or stalling until after the crisis is settled is a lost opportunity.

> *Tip: Crisis is an opportunity for breaking a stalemate.*

Recognizing the opportunity that comes with a crisis is not easy for the rejected parent. Timing or ripeness in response to the crisis is crucial if a spontaneous request for reunification occurs. Not knowing what is happening in their child's life is a serious obstacle for the rejected parent. The rejected parent is at a disadvantage unless the parent has access to information about what is happening in the child's life. The opportunity for reunification may come as a complete surprise because all communication between the rejected parent and the child had previously stopped. The correct timing for reunification usually comes about from an event that directly affects the child and to a lesser extent the parent. When the crisis occurs, some rejected parents are more receptive to reunification than others. Some rejected parents express fear of again being hurt by the child's rejection. The risk is too great. Some aligned parents who previously engaged in alienation were receptive to the reunification, but most were initially reluctant to allow the child to reconnect with the other parent.

How to motivate the rejecting child or the alienating parent and/or an estranging parent is a perplexing challenge for family courts and mental health professionals. Court orders are poor motivators for children or alienating parents to change their attitudes and feelings toward a rejected parent. Frequently parents obsessed in their desire to alienate are not intimidated by court orders or by the threat of contempt of court. Mental health professionals, with best intentions, become frustrated when their clients either refuse cooperation or sabotage reunification. Many courts are equally frustrated. They hear one contempt charge after another and make threats—only to see the parents in court again. The parents and sometimes the children then lose respect for the impotent court. Because of the court's failure to enforce court orders, some parents have made ethical complaints to the local bar association or the state's supreme court, alleging that the judge is incompetent for failing to sanction the offending parent. All too often, parents return to court for a contempt hearing only to hear the same order given again and again—and everyone involved knows that nothing will happen to change an obsessed parent's behavior.

Timing

Studies of crisis intervention demonstrate that psychological resistance to change will frequently dissolve when an individual, even a child, perceives that he or she is facing an emotionally charged crisis. Theory on international relations offers some valuable insight that is applicable toward motivating high-conflict parents and children for working cooperatively toward reunification (Kriesberg and Thorson 1991, Rubin 1991, Zartman 1989).

The concept of ripeness, defined as "a bilateral state of affairs, affecting both parties for the same reason," is relevant for understanding the timing for reunification (Pruitt and Olczak 1995). Conflicted parents and the alienated or estranged child can be ripe for reunification when there is a crisis. Ripeness is a common state of mind where both parents or a rejected parent and a rejecting child are motivated to avoid a shared crisis. A real-life example that I personally witnessed in a Virginia court was when the judge threatened to change the children's temporary custody to a trusted and neutral family member. The judge asked the attorneys to talk with their clients and ask for names of trusted friends or family members who could care for the children because the two parents could not work together for their children's best interest.. The threat worked to break the stalemate because all knew that the judge meant what he said. Both parents and the child would lose. The parents came to their senses and began working together.

Characteristic of ripeness is a common interest for a mutual outcome. The parents just described had a common interest because neither wanted the children displaced to a relative or family friend. They wanted the children to remain in a familiar and hopefully caring family environment.

Richard Gardner (2001) argued that forcing a change of custody from the alienating parent to the targeted parent would aid reunification. In his follow-up study, he reported improved relationships between the targeted parent and the children after the change of custody. He did not talk with the alienating parent because he was instrumental in the change of custody and expected a hostile reception. An alternative explanation for the reunification and perhaps the children's change in attitude was the crisis the judge created with the involuntary change of custody. The study would have had more value and perhaps offer greater insight if someone other than Dr. Gardner had interviewed both parents. What is unknown is the children's relationship with the alienating parent after the change of custody. I contend that successful reunification should include a positive relationship with both parents, not just with the targeted parent.

Zartman and Johannes (1991) described four circumstances when feuding parties are ripe or motivated to resolve their differences. Though the authors' discussion focuses on international conflicts, what they offer is applicable for high-conflict parents and for alienated or estranged children. These circumstances include a hurting stalemate, a recent catastrophe, an impending catastrophe or deteriorating position, and an enticing opportunity.

Hurting Stalemate

Both parents must come to the realization that they are in a "no win" situation, and if they persist in arguing their position, both parents as well as the child will suffer.

Jim's Story

Jim was like many sixteen-year-olds because he was impulsive and frequently displayed poor judgment. One evening while out with friends riding snowmobiles on the sixth green of the country club, he was arrested for destroying private property. Jim was panicky and wanted to find a way of escaping trouble. He remembered that his father was a trustee of the country club so Jim thought that his father might help him. He knew he needed help because he had already had a run-in with the sheriff in a separate incident.

Gingerly, he broached the idea with his mother about calling his father and asking for help. His mother was not happy with either Jim

---

or his idea. She told him, "That's up to you, but I don't like it. I know your father can help if he has a mind to." Mother had been frustrated because she felt for a long time that she had lost some control over Jim's behavior. She knew she needed help from Jim's father but did not know how to ask without risking an argument or the potential renewal of their protracted litigation.

Although Jim felt embarrassed, he made the call. His father was thrilled to hear Jim's voice again after an absence of four years. Wisely, Jim's father listened, withholding any judgment until he heard the full story. He knew that Jim was using him to get out of a scrape, but that was acceptable because he saw the opportunity to help his son and perhaps rebuild a relationship. Today, possibly for the first time in their relationship, Jim and his dad are connecting as father and son.

Prior to his parents' divorce Jim was estranged from his father because of his dad's lack of interest in his life. Jim recalled that his father was always either working or at the country club. Desperate for a relationship, Jim at the age of eight asked for a set of golf clubs because he wanted an avenue to connect with his dad. He got the clubs, but his father deferred his son's lessons to a pro rather than himself. One could only imagine Jim's disappointment. Like many estranged parents, Jim's father learned too late the value he placed on the relationship with his son. By the time this current crisis occurred, father and son had never played a round of golf together.

Following their divorce, Jim remembered his mother encouraging him to spend time with his father, but after several unsuccessful attempts to stay in touch with his dad, he and his mother gave up. Now she just feels contempt toward her ex-husband. She knows that Jim knows her feelings. She said that she no longer cared but the fact of the matter is she alienated Jim from his father, believing she was protecting her son from further hurt. She may have been right in her thinking but went too far by reinforcing, in Jim's thinking, all the reasons he should hate his father. She blames Jim's father for Jim being out of control. The incident at the country club was only one of many similar incidents. Jim was often oppositional to his mother's demands, and refused to follow her rules. She believed she had nowhere to turn to help her adolescent son. Both parents realized that they and Jim would all be losers if they continued fighting. They had to set aside their feelings to break the stalemate.

Jim's crisis broke the stalemate. Though his father knew his son was using him, he took advantage of the opportunity to reengage in his son's life. Jim's mother did not object to their contact and was openly relieved that there was a father to help her. She was wise to know that she had to contain her anger or risk pushing Jim away. She actively encouraged the father-son relationship to evolve naturally.

Recent Catastrophe

A shared crisis will bring people together who have been fighting for years. Science fiction movies have made use of this theme in the films *War of the Worlds* and, more recently, *Independence Day*. Both plots involved aliens who threatened the existence of the earth so the nations of the world united against a common enemy.

Natural catastrophes often bring out the best behavior even between strangers, each helping the other. People sharing a catastrophe or crisis will put differences aside for their common purpose. Hatred and hurts are prioritized to a less important status, at least for a time, so the individuals can work together, mutually supporting one another. Putting their other issues aside for a common purpose can resolve the crisis for the child's well-being.

Marta's Story

Marta learned from her adult brother and sister that her father, whom she had not seen for the last four of her nine years, was diagnosed with cancer. When she told her mother of her desire to see her father, she was told he was "a dirty, dangerous drunk who deserved to be sick and was not worthy of her compassion."

Marta decided to ask her siblings for help to see their father because she knew they had frequent contact with him and their stepmother. Also, the older children supported their father and their sister's desire to have a relationship. Her siblings began driving Marta to and from the visits without their mother's knowledge or consent.

When Marta's mother learned of the family conspiracy to reunite "her child" with her father, she immediately returned to court in an attempt to block reunification. Marta wrote a letter that her siblings gave to the judge hearing the case. In her letter she requested time with her father without jeopardizing her primary custodial residence with her mother, suggesting that her mother needed to have time for herself while she [Marta] spent time with her ailing dad.

The judge ordered access between father and daughter. Marta was given specific days each week when she could spend time with her father, usually in the company of her siblings. As the relationship progressed and the father's health deteriorated, her mother's heart softened so Marta was allowed to spend more time with her father. After her father's death, Marta wrote a thank-you letter to the judge for allowing her to have a relationship with her father before the opportunity was lost.

Though the court was ultimately involved in facilitating reunification, the crisis of the father's terminal illness motivated Marta to reach out to her father. Also, it is important to note that sometimes siblings can assist in initiating reunification. They can also be saboteurs.

Marta believed that her mother encouraged her to reject her father. She recalled a scene from her early childhood when her mother said to her father that she hated him. When her father accused her mother of "poisoning this child's mind," she physically stood between them and defiantly told her dad that it was all her idea and she wanted him out of her life. She could not remember her father ever doing anything toward her that caused her any discomfort or pain.

Impending Catastrophe or Deteriorating Position

Both parents are more likely to break their stalemate when they can foresee and agree that any inaction on their part will lead to an impending crisis for themselves and their child.

Jim and Casey's Story

For five years Jim and Casey had been fighting mostly on the telephone about financial problems and Jim's continued lack of contact with their

sixteen-year-old daughter, Stacy. The fighting had become a family rit-
ual because the hostilities were so predictable. While all this fighting
was going on, Casey did not notice the subtle changes in Stacy's mood.
She became more withdrawn and listless. She had little interest in what
used to be pleasurable activities. No longer was she invited to parties
and she didn't run to the phone for that very important phone call. Now
the phones were quiet, and the dresses hung undisturbed in the closet.
Casey was oblivious to what was happening to their daughter until she
received a call from the hospital that Stacy had seriously cut herself in
a suicide attempt.

Scared, Casey called Jim and met him at the hospital. Jim feared for
Stacy's life and could not contain himself from blaming Casey. Casey,
feeling defensive, counter-attacked with her own allegations. Like so
many times in the past, they lost control and could no longer see what
was important.

When the psychiatrist entered the waiting room, they eventually
stopped yelling and redirected their attention to him. The doctor stood
staring at them in disbelief. After Jim and Casey regained their composure, they were led into a small sterile-looking office beside the waiting
room. The doctor informed them that their daughter tried to kill herself
because she felt responsible for all the fighting, the multiple trips to
court, and the loss of her father from her life.

Immediately, Jim and Casey wanted to react, much like Pavlov's dogs,
with accusations and blame toward one another. Somehow, their wiser
instincts helped contain their impulses. They knew they had to listen to
what the doctor was saying. "Your daughter told me she wanted to die
because she couldn't stand to hear the two of you yelling and fighting,
and she did not want to grow up without her dad. The two of you need
to show your love for Stacy by putting your hostilities aside. Otherwise
you're going to lose her forever." This was the wake-up call they needed
to hear. They both understood that inaction could cost them both their
daughter's life.

Since her parents' separation and divorce, Stacy reported feeling both
alienated and estranged from her father and mother. Before and after her
time spent with her father, Stacy's mother would interrogate her about
conversations and activities with her father. During the interrogations,
Casey would make extremely negative comments about her father. In turn,
Jim asked questions about her mother. Both parents berated the other to

the point of her not knowing what to believe or who to love. She was tired of trying to defend one parent against the other.

Whenever her parents had contact with one another, they would fight, even on the telephone, so it just became easier and more peaceful not to see her father. However, that solution became emotionally unbearable for this adolescent so she placed all the blame for the family dysfunction on herself, leading to the suicide attempt.

Enticing Opportunity

An opportunity may arise for their child that demands the parents' co-operation. This requires the parents to think about what is best for the child rather than their own narcissistic needs. The opportunity may be completing the college financial statements for scholarships, planning for graduation, decisions about extensive medical treatment, or an important family event. For the narcissistically injured parent, he or she must feel a stronger empathy for the child's need rather than wallow in the pit of his or her own hurt or rage. This is very difficult for such parents.

Robert's Story

Robert has not seen his dad for ten years. His last memory of his parents together involved a great deal of yelling and screaming about something that was so insignificant he could not even remember what it was. He also knew his father was somewhere in the background most of his life. He did receive birthday cards and Christmas gifts every year but never a phone call. At times Robert would feel guilty for not responding after receiving a gift, but he learned early how to push those thoughts and feelings aside.

Now Robert was facing a dilemma. He needed money for college and knew that his mother couldn't help. Maybe Robert was mistaken, but he believed that his father was financially secure so he thought he might ask his dad for some tuition help. However, he knew that his proposal would anger his mother, but he was desperate for help to achieve his goal of a college education. So he decided to present the idea to his mother as a way of "getting more child support money from his father."

Robert's two older sisters were opposed to his plan. They were strongly aligned with their mother and had no contact with their father so the sisters did not believe their brother should call their dad. Both sisters pressured their mother to keep Robert away from their father.

However, with his mother's blessings, Robert decided to ask his father for help. His mother knew that might be the only way Robert could attend college. Robert could not blame his dad for being angry or for denying his request. He thought that his father might think he was just using him for money. The truth be known, yes. Robert told himself, "Go for it! What do I have to lose?" To Robert's surprise, his father was receptive, though he insisted on seeing Robert and setting some boundaries about how the money would be spent. Robert reluctantly agreed to his father's terms so this was now the beginning of a new relationship.

Success can take many forms, not just reconciliation but also a change in the parents' and child's beliefs or perceptions about each other. An example is Robert's realization that his father "is sometimes an ass, but I still care about him." Robert and his father may not have achieved a strong emotional bond, but both are satisfied that they can talk with each other and in a limited way be part of one another's lives. Some may not consider Robert and his father a success, but the son's change in his perception of his father is not a failure for either of them.

A parent's motivation to change can be for a variety of reasons. What occurred in a California court is an example of how a judge created a crisis for the parents, causing them to rethink their position.

A California family law judge encouraged parents to reach their own equitable parenting plan because he knew they would not be happy with his decision for their family. For one contentious couple he ordered them to negotiate for six weeks with a court-appointed mediator. They could meet with the mediator as many times as mutual scheduling would permit, but equitable access to their children for both parents was to be the goal.

The children demonstrated alienating behaviors toward both their parents. The mother's family was identified as the source of the alienation.

Because of the maternal family's interference, the parents were frustrated by the stalemate. They feared for the children because they knew that the children were headed toward court-ordered temporary foster care. To divert a crisis and to avoid causing further harm to the children, a member of the father's family agreed to care for the children in the family home. Everyone agreed to allow this family member to care for the children because they knew the consequences to the children if an agreement could not be reached. The threat that the children would be placed in foster care was very real, for they knew the judge's reputation for not bluffing. The mutual agreement was the first step in breaking the stalemate.

While the children stayed with the family member, the court ordered reunification coaching for the father and both parents together had supervised visitation. Prior to the first visit, they were given specific instructions about how to reestablish the bond and reduce the children's anxieties. The parents were specifically told during the visits to not discuss with one another, in the children's presence, adult (ex-spousal) issues but instead to focus on playing a game and praising their children's successes. The children had to personally observe their parents calmly communicating together for their best interest. If either parent erred in these ways, the visit was terminated.

The judge's order and threat to put the children in foster care effectively gave the parents reasons for putting their differences aside. He created circumstances for motivating the parents and extended family to change because the crisis then had more to do with the children than the parents' need to control. They all saw a potential crisis looming for the children. The parents and extended family were put in a hurting stalemate because they and their children were in a "no win" situation unless they cooperated with each other. With the threat of foster care, the parents and the children shared the potential of an impending catastrophe, and without a shared solution each was placed in a deteriorating position. To avoid the crisis, the court provided an enticing opportunity for these parents by offering the pathway to resolution through mediation and reunification therapy.

Parents entrenched in their own irrational beliefs about what is best for the children will resist change. The irrational belief can be "my child doesn't need a father." This is especially true for parents who are obsessed about destroying the children's relationship with the targeted parent. Obsessed parents can be completely absorbed with their own need to control while failing to see how their behavior harms the children. A crisis that somehow causes the obsessed parent to feel deeply for the child's impending pain can motivate them to step back and see what their obstinate behavior is doing to the children.

There is a lot to be learned from these parents and children about how to motivate a noncompliant parent. Rather than waiting for a crisis, the court may need to consider creating its own crisis for the alienating parents. There are several ways courts can create a crisis.

- Make a recommendation for a change of custody to the targeted parent for failing to comply with court orders. The alienating parent should know before going to court that the court might make this recommendation. Fear can be an effective motivator for change.

- The court orders both parents to sit in county jail long enough to understand the consequences for failing to comply with court orders. The trip to jail would not be an arrest but instead a wake-up call that the judge is serious.

- Require the alienating parent to put a significant sum of money in an escrow account to pay for missed counseling appointments, court expenses for the compliant parent, and other costs associated with noncompliances.

- File criminal charges for contempt and allow a plea bargain to include cooperation with court orders. West Virginia recently (2008) passed a law criminalizing false allegations of abuse in the context of custody litigation. The penalty can be a fine up to a thousand dollars and/or community service. In time, more states may follow West Virginia's lead.

- The court or a parent coordinator having arbitration power orders the target parent additional parenting time to begin on the day of the hearing.

For the crisis to work, the court must not be bluffing. The court must follow through with the threat and realize that the court will be the target of the alienating parent's rage. The sanctions, if possible, should occur immediately. What happens in many jurisdictions is that parents do not take the court's threats seriously. Courts can get a reputation of being all talk and no action.

Courts have reason to be concerned that the alienating parent will have more reason to blame the targeted parent for the court's actions. The alienating parent can be heard to say, "See what your father is doing to me.

He is sending me to jail. I told you he is dangerous and has no concern for your feelings." To counter the assertion, the judge should insist that he or she talk to the child and explain to the child that the order comes from the court and not from the parents. Sanctions should be imposed on both parents equally, thereby defusing any blame.

The actions of the court must not hurt the children. The court and not the targeted parent must take the blame for the court's decision. This has to be emphasized to both the parents and the children. Second, the alienating parent has to be frightened by the prospect of the order. He or she must feel the emotional impact of the crisis. There must be an escape clause in the court order that specifically describes to the parents the court's expectations and how they can avoid the court's sanctions with proper action. The parents need to know that if they do such and such, they will avoid the adverse consequences that are described in the court order.

Finding a way to motivate warring parents to change their behaviors and attitudes seems next to impossible, especially when the parents sound more interested in destroying each other with accusations and faultfinding. No one will disagree with the argument that parents need to get along for their children's welfare, but this argument is too often ignored during the heat of the battle.

4

Obstacles to Change:
Symbolic Communication

Communication is a skill to learn. We learn from our parents, friends, and those we look up to. Our innate personality influences how we perceive, interpret, and react to the world around us. While your marriage deteriorates, your communication skills will falter. You may struggle with uncertainty and question your own competency to face the challenges ahead. Adapting to the stress caused by realigning the family and coping with an impartial judicial system requires new skills.

Parents yelling or screaming, walking away from each other in frustration, or just avoiding talking to each other, behave this way because they fail to understand some of the intricacies involved with effective communication. Much of this error is avoided when you recognize the pitfalls that disrupt effective communication.

During the course of any conversation between two people, there are two threads of information occurring at the same time: the message or topic discussed, and how the message is delivered. If you stand back and watch two people argue, you can quickly identify the topic of the argument. Most people believe that the topic or difference of opinion is the cause of their emotional reaction. This is not always true. Frequently, the other person's yelling or loss of control—and not the issue discussed—will trigger your emotions. People usually react intensely to a person's delivery. If you yell, call me names, or walk out, my emotions are driven more by your behavior than by what you say. If I stop focusing my attention on the topic but instead react to your delivery, you can bet the issue will not get resolved.

Common obstacles to effective communication that lead to unresolved fights, misunderstandings, and hurt feelings, are symbolic miscommunication, boundary issues, blame, theorizing, and ex-spousal issues. You can expect to see one or more of these obstacles when dysfunctional high-conflict parents argue. Learning to recognize your dysfunctional obstacles and then knowing how to change your behavior will improve your ability to communicate and work with the other parent and your children. Everyone benefits when you learn how to recognize the obstacles when they are occurring, how to respond to the other person's dysfunctional communication, and how to improve your personal communication skills.

Symbolic Communication

"I don't know why you are making such a big deal of my forgetting Jimmy's birthday. I'll get a birthday gift before our next visit. He'll understand, even if you don't."

During the latter months of a failing marriage, parents tread gingerly about the house, being sensitive to the silent nuances of each other's behavior, hoping to pick up any cues that may warn them of an impending skirmish. A tone of voice or a harsh stare serves warning to keep your distance. The tension will hover over the house until someone has the misfortune of triggering the inevitable quarrel. Once the fight begins, there is no retreat from the rapid escalation of hostilities. The skirmish never seems to get resolved. Instead, the hostilities slowly subside because fatigue sets in, or you retreat after feeling beaten down by the other's assault. With the return of uneasy calm, you promise yourself to never lose control again. You may even rehearse in your mind a strategy for preventing the next battle, knowing in your heart that your attempts will fail. You are confused, but hopeful that the next fight can be avoided.

It is a mistake to believe that parents will no longer argue after the divorce is final. Arguments between parents may actually get worse, though the issues change. Parents continue to fight because old habits are hard to break, hurts continue to fester, and they continue to lack the necessary skills to talk out their differences. This may have been part of the reason for the divorce. Another reason that is rarely talked about and not understood well is the role of symbols that ignite hostilities. Skirmishes, like those described above, are often a clue that someone has triggered a symbolic issue. Symbolic communication is perhaps one of the more difficult concepts to understand, but is essential if you are going to minimize alienation.

What Is Symbolic Communication?

Every day we rely on symbols to communicate with each other. The size of a tip tells the waitress how we value her service; forgoing a golf game to be with the family says "you are important"; wearing a black negligee suggests "I'm interested." These are all examples of symbolic communication. A symbol is any object or activity that has a special meaning and stirs an emotional reaction more intense than is warranted by the object's intrinsic value.

Who has custody has tremendous symbolic significance. We still live in a sexist society. If a father fights for custody and loses, he is thought of as an excellent and loving father who got screwed by the system. Mother loses custody and she is viewed as if something were wrong with her. This is not equality. This is one reason that shared parenting is a good idea. For a noncustodial mother to say she has shared parenting has less stigma than saying "I lost custody." Who has physical custody is very symbolic and influences how the parent is perceived. Many noncustodial parents are very self-conscious about how they are judged by others. This is not just a father's issue.

....

Tip: Symbols can be irrational:

....

While a family is breaking up, both the children and parents learn that particular behaviors, various activities, and possessions that were once taken for granted now have new symbolic significance. Giving a rose to someone you love is an example of how an object takes on a symbolic meaning. For most women and some men, the rose is symbolic of love. Instead, imagine receiving two dollars from someone you love and being told that they decided to give you the money rather than a rose because the rose will die. Will the two dollars have the same meaning? Of course not. The two dollars has more intrinsic value but the rose has more symbolic value. Your reaction to the two dollars will be very different from your reaction to the rose. Receiving the rose would bring the two of you closer while the two dollars may actually be offensive or taken as a joke. Why is there such a difference in the way someone would react? The reason is that people in our culture have learned that a rose has a symbolic meaning beyond being a pretty flower. It symbolizes care and love. A rose may have different meanings in different cultures.

You cannot be expected to worry about everything you say or do as you go through life, especially during a divorce. However, a divorce requires you to be more sensitive because everyone can be on edge. Instead, you will avoid many problems if you learn to recognize new symbols that become apparent during a divorce or separation. Divorce and separation are an impetus for new symbols.

Children also have symbols—breaking a simple promise to take them to get ice cream, or forgetting a special birthday gift can symbolize to the child "not caring." Understanding symbols will help you prevent a lot of confusion and hurt for your children. Children can be very sensitive to any signs of rejection during the divorce. They need reassurance that both parents love them. An alienating parent can take advantage of your child's sensitivity by telling the child how they should interpret the targeted parent's behavior. The alienating parent's interpretation may have nothing to do with reality and instead may be the alienating parent's projection.

"Mom, is Dad going to be late again?"

"What do you think? He's always late."

"I don't know if I should call Robbie and see if he wants to come out and play"

"You need to just sit and wait. You know how angry he gets if you are not ready. If he really cared about you, he wouldn't be late all the time."

To help you better understand and identify symbols, you may want to complete the following exercise.

Exercise: Identifying Symbols

Remember the definition of a symbol: any object or activity that evokes an emotional reaction greater than the activity's or object's intrinsic worth. Begin by remembering an incident when you or someone close to you had an intense emotional reaction that appeared to be out of control. Now, having the incident in mind, think about what the incident could have meant to the person having the emotional reaction. To help you, consider this example:

Joyce got angry and began yelling when Terry offered to install her storm windows. Terry thought Joyce's reaction was out of line because she needed help and he only wanted to help her prepare for winter.

Joyce's anger appeared out of proportion and suggested to Terry that his offer had a symbolic meaning for Joyce. At this point, Terry can only guess the meaning behind her reaction. She may have thought that Terry's offer was a put-down, suggesting she can't take care of herself, or a reminder of her dependence on him.

List on a piece of paper other examples of symbols and your thoughts about the possible meanings behind them. After completing your list, think of new symbols that have come to light since the divorce.

This exercise, which I am sure you will agree, is difficult. An individual's intense reaction that is grossly out of proportion is a cue that you are dealing with something symbolic. Your ability to recognize both your and the other person's symbols should cause you to pause and take a moment to think about how to respond to the intense feelings. You may change your strategy or be more deliberate in what you say, either of which will help avoid an argument.

Tip: Symbols are learned:

Learning symbols begins in infancy. The first smile and deliberate eye contact you make with someone conveys love and warmth. Everyone learns a cluster of symbols that continually change with age and time. A mother's smile directed toward her child communicates approval. Father's pat on the back says, "I'm proud of you." Symbols vary from one culture and subculture to another. Much of the discomfort of beginning a new job or getting a divorce is learning a new array of symbols, so that no one is offended. You learn the symbols of power and authority, proper timing, and acceptable channels of communication. Even the way you dress has symbolic meaning. Ask any teenager about the importance of having a cell phone and text messaging.

A person's age, a change in circumstances, and timing all influence the symbolic importance placed on an object or an activity. A teenager will often feel slighted when he or she rides in a friend's car and is asked to sit in the back seat. Riding "shot gun" has a special status. A teen staying home on Friday and Saturday night, having nowhere to go, is the worst yet. Not going out on the weekend is symbolic of not being popular. When the teen grows to adulthood, staying home on Friday night is much less important because the symbolism no longer exists. The adult is now more concerned about his comfort than the status of sitting in the front seat of a car or the shame of not having a weekend date. There is a lot to be said about getting older. A lot of what was once important is now not a big deal.

Newly divorced parents quickly learn that their unique clusters of symbols change. Behavior that was once acceptable may now be offensive. No longer can you safely assume that your ex-spouse will approve of your behavior. Making matters more confusing is that symbols are very similar to boundary issues.

"What makes you think you can just walk into my house and go to the refrigerator and get yourself a beer?"

"This is still my house and my refrigerator. I can come and go as I please."

"No, you can't. I can't just walk into your apartment and help myself to whatever I want. And, I don't want you to think you can just go into my purse and take some money. That is offensive."

"What is the big deal? I have always gone into your purse to get money and you never complained before."

"We weren't getting a divorce before. Now it's offensive. Please stay out of my purse. If you need money, ask me and don't just assume you can take it."

Each individual gives each object or activity its own unique value or significance. When Jessie sees her ex-husband take a beer from her refrigerator, her reaction is intense. Jessie immediately perceives his behavior as inappropriate and offensive. She probably didn't care that much about the beer (symbol) or even the money but was offended by her ex-husband's presumption that he could go into her refrigerator and help himself (boundary). Going into the refrigerator and taking the beer or the purse to take money is the context that gives meaning to the beer and money and may symbolize for Jessie a lack of respect and an unwanted familiarity. Many times, violating a person's symbol is also a violation of boundaries. Notice that the example demonstrates strong feelings felt by the person who is reacting to a symbol (beer and money) and a boundary violation (the act of taking the beer from the refrigerator and the money from the purse). Her ex-husband's reaction is usually not to the symbol but instead to Jessie's intense reaction. He may think that her reaction is irrational or ridiculous. That is why it is so hard to win an argument with a person who is reacting to a symbol.

Learning to identify symbols is helpful in preventing alienation and resolving conflicts between you and your ex-spouse. Once you have identified a symbol, you must realize that you are not going to change how the person feels about the symbolic object or act. You cannot expect to change another person's symbolic interpretation; whether or not the symbol is irrational makes no difference. You will only make matters worse if you try to convince someone that their symbols are arbitrary and less important than they think. Pushing the issue will only cause the other person to get defensive and angry. Instead, listen to what the person is saying and try to negotiate your difference of opinion. To keep the peace, you may have to compromise your position after realizing that the issue is not that important to you. If you are lucky, you and your ex-spouse do not have the conflicting symbols, otherwise you may need professional help or mediation to work out your differences.

"I don't care if you want a beer or need a few dollars, just ask. Give me that respect."

"I shouldn't have to ask to come into my own house."

"But you have to. That is the court order. Fighting with me will only make matters worse. It's not good for our children to hear us fight. I admit that I get offended and angry. Then I don't want to do anything to help you. Please, just ask."

"Jessie, do you know what that feels like, having to ask? That's humiliating."

"I don't want to humiliate you. I know this is hard for everyone. But for our children's sake, we must not fight."

This example may be simplistic but there are a couple of points worth considering. When there is a court order, the order is a reality that both parents must live with, like it or not, unless they choose to return to court. Secondly, Jessie has a right to remind her ex-husband about the boundaries and she did so without humiliating or verbally attacking. The boundary of not just walking into the house and helping yourself is very real. Violating the boundary is offensive. For the father, being told that he can't walk into the house uninvited is symbolic of the rejection and perhaps emasculates him. It is a reminder of the rejection that he may have felt. Both parents started to empathize with how the other feels with criticism. They were talking about how they personally felt rather than attacking the other parent. This is an important first step to working together.

Recognize that adult symbols can be confusing and difficult to learn. You may have some idea that you are reacting to a symbol when you later think back to an argument and can't remember what you fought about, or you conclude that what you were fighting about was stupid. You could have reacted to the person's delivery rather than a specific topic. When you figure out that what you are fighting about is a symbol, your best strategy is to back off and let the tensions cool because you will never win. At best, the two of you will beat each other down until one of you quietly surrenders. Of course when this happens, the issue is not resolved.

If you listen carefully to an argument between two ex-spouses, you will often hear one trying to convince the other to change the value of their symbols.

"Mary, what time is Robbie's birthday party? I don't want to be late."

"I don't want you to come. I have arranged for his party and if you want a party, you need to have a party on your time, not mine."

"That isn't fair. Robbie is my son too."

"Ramone, I don't care."

"How do you think Robbie will feel? He asked if I will be at his party and I told him I would be there."

"I don't care. That is between you and Robbie."

"Robbie will think I broke a promise (symbol) and don't care about him."

"You should have thought about that before saying you will be at the party."

"How do you think Robbie will feel when I don't show up at the party? He'll think I am a liar because I broke my promise or I don't care about him."

"You need to discuss that with Robbie."

Ramone is frustrated and angry by Mary's refusal to allow him to attend their son's birthday party (symbol of love and being a good father). He may theorize in his mind that, "She doesn't want me around because she is jealous about my relationship with Robbie." Mary argues, "You don't live here anymore (boundary issue). Can't you get that in your mind? If you want, have your own birthday party but leave me alone." Because of their intense feelings, we know that Ramone's attendance at Robbie's birthday party has a symbolic meaning for both. Ramone may believe that not being at his son's party will make him less of a loving parent in his child's eyes. His son may share the same belief. Mary believes that Ramone's insistence on attending the party is his way of controlling her, an attempt to deny that the relationship is over. I suspect that the son would like a peaceful party with both parents in attendance. The son is the loser in this unresolved situation.

At times like this, parents must remember that children observe and remember how their parents behave. The parents are the children's role models. Children adjust better to divorce with parents (Amato 1993, Berg and Kelly 1979) who are able to calmly converse with each other. If Ramone and Mary are going to work out their differences, they must begin by realizing that neither one of them will back down because they cannot agree with the other person's view. If they continually throw insults at each other, they will do nothing more than incite a fight. Instead, parents must learn to tolerate the other's symbols and negotiate a compromise about whether Ramone should or should not attend the party. Both parents must remember what is best for Robbie rather than only thinking about themselves.

Tip: Differences in symbols may incite an argument, but the person's delivery is what usually keeps the fight going.

Tip: Working with Symbols

- *Begin by recognizing a symbolic issue. You can tell when a person's verbiage is more intense than what seems reasonable.*

- *You cannot reason with a person until the person calms down and speaks with a normal tone of voice. Focus on reducing the tension rather than resolving the issue. You may suggest, "Let's talk about this later." If you make this suggestion, set a time and place to talk about the issue. "Could we talk about this on the phone after we calm down and Robbie goes to bed?" Agree ahead of time to stick with the single issue and not bring other issues into the discussion. "Can we agree to just stay focused on your coming to Robbie's party?"*

- *When tensions are calmed, try to find a compromise, knowing that neither of you will be completely satisfied. Keep in mind that if you get what you want, you must give something in return; this is only fair.*

- *If the issue is important and there is no compromise, consider mediation or a counselor.*

Tip: Money and child support can be symbolic:

Money is probably the most powerful symbol in our culture; it represents power. We hear this during election time when there is discussion about lobbyists and how money buys votes. Money, or the lack of it, is often a weapon that parents use against each other. Money is often the reason for parent's frequent return to court.

Child support is perhaps the most sensitive issue parents will address before the divorce is final. The noncustodial parent, whether the father or mother, will be required to pay a determined amount of money to their ex-spouse monthly. Men paying support continue to be the norm. Women paying support has a different feeling. That difference is the symbolism. The amount of child support is an emotional issue. The size of the payment has both a symbolic and a practical significance to both parents. Both parents are keenly aware that their standard of living and the amount of their discretionary money is dramatically reduced because of the divorce. Before going to court, parents may have heard horror stories of how both custodial and noncustodial parents have been shafted by the court. The parent, usually the father having to pay child support, may hear rumors that support has gone through the roof. These rumors evoke bitterness even before the parents enter the courtroom. The father imagines a future of living in a dingy three-room apartment while his ex-spouse and children continue to live in the marital home with a new car in the garage and the ex-wife's boyfriend mowing the lawn. To make matters worse, the boyfriend is probably using the father's self-propelled, self-mulching lawnmower. These images may not have a shred of truth, but they provoke intense bitterness.

Rational Belief: After the divorce, both parents' standard of living will likely be reduced.

Support payments are not an easy issue for the custodial parent either. They have their worries too. They know that they will be financially dependent upon their ex-spouse for many years to come. They worry about whether their ex-spouse will lose their job, continue to pay support, whether the check arrives on time, or if they will have money for financial emergencies. All these worries remind the custodial parent of their vulnerability and dependency upon their ex-spouse. He or she feels threatened by the ex-spouse's power, knowing that the money can dry up at any time. Each month when the check is due, there is another reminder of the past that they cannot shed.

Tip: Possessions can be symbolic.

After a divorce, a child's possessions may take on a new symbolic significance for either parent. A toy or an article of clothing may have an emotional value worth far more than the intrinsic value of the object. The object could be the child's security blanket, a computer game, a doll, or toy cars. The toy may trigger a parent's thoughts about betrayal, envy, or power. The idea that an article of clothing would stay at the other parent's home may arouse strong feelings that may appear irrational to an observer. In such instances, ask yourself, "What symbolic meaning does the object have for me?" Is the coat or the money for a church activity worth the fight? There are many possible symbolic meanings that a child's possession may have for a parent.

A well-meaning parent is risking alienation if he buys expensive gifts for the children without the other parent's support. The expensive gift can remind the other parent of her financial loss from the divorce or her inadequacy for not being able to give a toy of similar value. Before making an expensive purchase, think about the consequences for your children and their relationship with their other parent. Giving the expensive gift may make you a hero in your children's eyes, but remember the illusion is short-lived. Other consequences may last longer.

When your ex-spouse buys your children expensive gifts, don't agonize over the idea that he is buying your children's love. Grandparents frequently buy gifts without threatening our child's love. Unfortunately, there is not much you can do about the gifts. You will probably make matters worse if you try to stop the other parent or expect the child to not use the gift. Instead, have more faith and trust the strength of the relationship with your children. When your child feels and trusts your love and acceptance, the other parent will not destroy those feelings with expensive gifts. True, children are influenced by possessions, but as they get older, the quality of relationships and experiences will mean more. The immediate thrill of a new possession does not last long—not as long as how the child feels seeing his two parents fighting. Look back on your own fond memories of your parents.

Robert and Lisa

Robert bought his eight-year-old son a motorized dirt bike, despite his ex-wife's objections. Though Lisa may have good reason for her disapproval, the bike was a symbol of Robert's contempt for her authority. She was angry and frustrated, knowing she was powerless to do anything about the gift. She knew she could not say too much to her son because he would either ignore her plea to not ride the bike or see her as the bad guy. Talking to her ex-husband was useless because he had already made his point: "I don't care what you think."

Tip: Clothing and toys can be symbolic.

Parents may argue about children taking their possessions back and forth between households. "I bought the clothes, they stay here," says one mother. Some parents use the child's property as a ploy to hurt the other parent. Refusing to allow the child to take a favorite doll or coat may be an opportunity for a parent to say to the child, "He keeps the good clothes and returns junk" or "If you take that home, I'll never see it again." Hearing the allegation, the child is supposed to blame the other parent for not being able to take her favorite coat. Sometimes this alienating tactic will backfire, causing the child to feel estranged from the complaining parent.

Children do not want to be part of their parents' battles. Instead, a child should be allowed to transport toys or inexpensive clothing between homes as long as they are properly cared for and returned. Large toys, such as a bike, can be a problem and may not be practical to transport between homes. If expensive jewelry is likely to cause problems with the other parent or there is a fear that the jewelry could be lost, it is best not to give the jewelry to the child until he or she is older and more responsible. It is unfair to expect the other parent to be responsible for such a gift. Another problem is the gift of a pet, and expecting that the child will take the pet to the other household without asking first. The other parent may not have the room, interest, or resources to care for a pet and therefore should not be expected to care for the animal without first asking. Do not expect the child to do the asking.

Tip: Managing Toys and Possessions

- *Children should be allowed to have some choice about what they take to the other home.*
- *Do not give your child a toy or clothing that is not age appropriate. It is not fair to give the other parent responsibility for taking care of something valuable when they didn't agree it was age appropriate for the child. An example would be a motor bike for a three-year-old.*
- *If your children cannot properly care for a toy without close supervision, do not have them take the toy on a visit.*
- *Do not allow your children to take a toy to the other home if it requires close adult supervision without first getting the other parent's approval. An example is letting your ten-year-old take a chemistry set or a gun. The other parent may resent having to supervise the activity or may disagree with your values about what is an appropriate gift. Do not be afraid to say no to your children. That is part of being a parent.*
- *If parents can't stop arguing over clothing, it may be a good idea for each parent to have their own set of clothing. Be sure to return the clothes the children wore when they arrived at your home.*
- *During the winter, both parents should share the children's winter jackets or boots. Having two sets of outerwear does not always make sense for many families with limited money.*
- *Your children should return home from a parenting time wearing clean clothes. If they can't because they are returning from the beach or someplace where they get dirty, warn the other parent about what to expect.*

Tip: Do not expect your child to resolve clothing issues. This should be the parents' responsibility.

Parents should settle their differences about possessions between themselves without the children's involvement or hearing an argument. It is fine to ask their opinions about what they would like to bring, but you need to make the decision. Before fighting with your child about clothes, think about whether the clothing is worth the fight. This could be one of those symbolic issues discussed earlier. It may not be worth fighting about a dress, a blanket, or a video game if all you do is upset everyone with your words, including yourself.

....
Tip: Timing can be symbolic.
....

Timing is an important concept when trying to understand symbolic communication and alienation. An activity that occurs at one particular time may have an entirely different symbolic meaning at another time. To illustrate the concept, consider the effects of timing when teaching your children about good and bad touch. Parents will take the time to teach the children this concept when they are old enough to understand. The explanation is a warning to the children not to allow anyone to touch their "private parts." If anyone attempts to touch the private parts, they are instructed to say "No!" and immediately tell their parents. Teaching good and bad touch is appropriate but the timing can cause misunderstanding.

Imagine how different the symbolic meaning of your teachings would be to your children if you initially instruct them on good and bad touch just before they go on their first visit with their father. Your timing could suggest to the children that there may be something seriously wrong with their father, that he is dangerous, and should not be trusted. Although you are not intending to alienate the children from their father, your timing may have a symbolic connotation suggesting they are at risk.

Eleanor and Tom

"I wish you would say what you mean!" were Eleanor's departing words to Tom. Tom had bitterly left Eleanor's house before without the children. Tom persisted because he didn't want this to happen again. "I don't see what the big deal is if I'm a little late. I said I would be here at four o'clock. It's four twenty—so what?" Feeling empowered, Eleanor stood firm. Tom was helpless because he knew he could not do a thing about Eleanor's tenacity, for now.

"The custody agreement says four o'clock Saturday, not any time after four o'clock or whenever you feel like arriving," she declares. In turn, she informs the children that their dad must not really want to see them. "If he did," she says, "he'd be here on time."

When Tom retaliates by taking Eleanor back to court (for the fourth time in two years), she tells the judge that her ex-husband's lateness

---

"upsets the children terribly" and brings along their daughter Angela to corroborate the claim. Her parting words to the nine-year-old as she goes in to testify against her dad are, "I know you love me and would never let me down."

Is Eleanor being irrational? Why would she feel that twenty minutes is so important when her defiance will force a return to court and publicly revive the animosities with Tom? The issue is not Tom being late, but his tardiness has a symbolic meaning for Eleanor. This is apparent because the intensity of Eleanor's feelings is greater than what most people would feel in a similar situation. True, Tom's chronic tardiness can be a nuisance and perhaps is inexcusable, but is it worth going to court? There are many possibilities about what Tom's tardiness could mean to Eleanor. She may feel incensed by what she believes is Tom's lack of respect for her time, his blatant refusal to comply with her demand that he be on time, or a reminder of his lackadaisical attitude that helped destroy the marriage. Any time a person like Eleanor appears to be overly reacting to an activity or an event, the person is probably reacting to the symbol rather than the activity's or the event's intrinsic value. The flip side of this example is the possibility that Tom is unconsciously aware of the symbolic significance to Eleanor of his being late. His tardiness could be motivated by his desire to get back at Eleanor by inciting her rage. If so, he must step back and consider his son's feelings. There is no excuse for Tom's behavior if that is his intention. He needs to be more empathetic even if he is an individual who is chronically late for everything. There are some people like that. Eleanor would know if Tom was always late, even before the marriage went bad.

Tip: Working with Timing

- *Being sensitive to proper timing will avoid a lot of arguments.*
- *Don't drop a bombshell on your children or ex-spouse and expect to walk away without any discussion. You are asking for trouble when you do this.*
- *When you ask a favor or a change in the parenting time schedule, give the other person time to think about your request. If you expect an immediate answer to something that is important or requires sacrifice, you will likely hear a "No!" You are*

more likely to get cooperation if you let the person think about your request before responding. You may also want to consider what you are willing to give in order to get the parent's cooperation.

- *Give your children and ex-spouse time to plan.*
- *Surprise changes in plans will usually cause problems for both your children and your ex-spouse. Being predictable and consistent will strengthen their trust in you.*
- *Don't expect your children to negotiate time changes. This should be done between you and the other parent. Keep the children from getting between the two of you.*
- *Expect animosity from your ex-spouse and children if you frequently cancel or change parenting time.*
- *You can expect trouble if you show up unexpectedly at your ex-spouse's home without an invitation.*

Tip: Activities can be symbolic.

When the court dictates to noncustodial parents how and when they are to spend time with their children, it is common for the parent to feel enraged because their power to choose when to see the children has been eroded. The court's declaration can be symbolically interpreted by the parent to mean "I'm no longer important to my children." In turn, this gives the custodial parent tremendous power because they become the child's gatekeeper. Some parents abuse this power and use it as a way to vent their anger toward the rejected parent. The symbolic interpretation of "You are no longer important to your children" causes parent's excruciating pain and bitterness. Blame for the decision is often placed on the other parent even though he or she did not make the decision. To make matters worse, the noncustodial parent often sees the court giving the custodial parent all the power, the power to give or take away permission to see the children or attend their activities. To some extent, this is true. The noncustodial parent can no longer come and go as he or she pleases. Symbolic issues around the sharing of activities will not be dealt with by court orders alone. Courts cannot dictate a cooperative attitude, happy feelings, or a parent's sincerity in wanting the other parent involved in the children's lives. Appreciating the importance of both parents being active participants in the children's lives must come from the parents themselves.

Martha and Tony

Both Martha and Tony are proud of Kenny's accomplishment as a soccer player. Now, the dreaded awards banquet is coming up and all are reminded of the spectacle that happened last year. Martha was enraged about Tony wanting to sit at their table, believing that he should have his own table because he is no longer part of her family. She publicly let her feelings be known to all, especially Kenny. Her yelling was a spectacle that was embarrassing to Tom and Kenny.

Take a moment and think about how Kenny and his father felt after Martha berated Tony publicly. What should Tony do? Insist on sitting at Martha's table? Leave the banquet? Go to another table? What was Martha reacting to? Who has the power? What can both parents do to make things better for Kenny? Most importantly, what could have been done to prevent this confrontation?

Martha and Tony's confrontation is an example of how one incident can trigger hard feelings because of what the incident symbolizes for each parent. Tony's unexpected intrusion may remind Martha of his presumption that he can do whatever he wants without asking. She remembers the many times during the marriage when he tried to control her. "Tony could care less about my feelings. All he was interested in was doing what he wanted. Well, he isn't going to run over me again."

Tony also has his symbolic issues. He is hurt by Martha's abrupt rejection and the humiliating thought of sitting alone while his son is sitting at the next table. He is furious at Martha's reminder that she has the power to dictate where he is not allowed to sit. Rejection was not new for Tony. He recalls how "the bitch has always tried to interfere with the relationship with my son. Now I'm supposed to be happy relegated to a 'nobody.'"

The interaction between parents, when one has to ask the other for permission to see their children or attend an activity, can be a symbolic trigger that ignites old hurts and hostilities for both parents. The parent asking for an extra eight hours may think, "What right does she or the court have telling me when I can be a father to my kids?" He is reminded that some of the rewards of being a father can be taken away, like being able to spontaneously ask his children, "Would you like to go and get an ice cream?"

Worse yet is the belief that something is wrong with him because he wants to spend more time with his kids. While attempting to regain parenting time, one parent said, "I no longer have any credibility. I am a nothing! I have no relevance to my boys. The court has taken away everything that has meaning to me because I was once depressed. I give up."

Exchanging the children or showing up unexpectedly at an activity are the times when parents are at greatest risk to trigger intense feelings caused by some symbolic meaning of the parent's appearance. Parents often sense this, even if they cannot explain it. Children, too, feel the tension. Parents need to realize that the exchange is a risky time that requires a concerted effort to not pick a fight and instead make the exchange as pleasant as possible. They must remember that the children may also be uncomfortable because the exchange becomes their symbol of the divorce and a reminder of the parents' animosity.

Tip: Recall what Cesar Millan, the Dog Whisperer, says about how you influence others by the energy you radiate. This is very true for children during the exchanges. Your child's resistance or emotional shutdown could have more to do with the energy he or she is feeling than the idea of going with the other parent.

Courts recognize the importance of encouraging the noncustodial parent's involvement with their children. Children want both parents involved with their school or extracurricular activities. They want to believe they can hug and kiss both parents without them worrying about how the other parent will react. When the custodial parent interferes with the other parent's opportunity to share in the children's activities, the children may feel frustrated and bitter, perhaps thinking they have been snubbed or rejected. The children may falsely accuse the noncustodial parent of not caring. Parents refusing or forgetting to give the other parent advance notice of their children's activities are risking alienation.

Courts can help prevent timing problems. When the court learns that the parents are unable to talk out their differences or one parent abuses their gatekeeping power, the court orders need to be very specific about the allocation of parental rights and responsibilities. Ordering "liberal visitation" does not work with these parents. Court orders need to be very structured until the parents can learn to work together.

Understanding symbolic communication will take you a long way to understanding and preventing alienation. It is not always easy to know what to do when you see the emotional outburst that comes after violating something that is symbolically important to another person. It requires both you and your ex-spouse to be patient and forgiving of each other for the other's mistakes. Try to remember that attacking hurts everyone, especially the children, who are less able to control and emotionally defend themselves against the hurt. Learn to respect each other's symbols, learn to prioritize what is most important to your children, learn to negotiate your differences, and be patient and forgiving.

Obstacles to Change: Blaming

Blaming occurs when you accuse someone of an offense. Your accusation can be based on your personal experience or what you theorize to explain your child's behavior.. Blaming and theorizing can go hand in hand. When you don't like what's happening and don't understand why something is happening that is distressing, an initial inclination may be to theorize and blame someone, usually the ex-spouse. This is very common practice even when alienation is not an issue. Children's behavior is not always rational and easy to explain. Many times the child's oppositional behavior is a normal part of the child's development. The error in the parent's thinking is to blame the other parent for the child's misbehavior rather than seeing the child's behavior as a normal parenting issue. Parenting is never easy. It is more difficult if you maintain the irrational belief that all of your child's misbehavior is the ex-spouse's fault. Your anger and frustration will intensify if you wait for the ex-spouse to fix your child's misbehavior. That is not going to happen. You have to take some responsibility and act. Some of these statements below may sound familiar.

"It's your fault that Billy doesn't visit."

"Look at how *you* are hurting Billy with all your yelling. Get control of yourself!"

"Would you just shut up, so I don't have to listen to *your* yelling."

"You are the reason Robbie is failing spelling. You don't study with him."

"*You* never listen to what I have to say."

"It's your selfishness why Billy doesn't want to see you."

Do any of these statements sound familiar? You can see why a parent would get defensive and react with little hope for resolution. Blaming and verbal attacks add fuel to the fire causing each parent to get defensive and ready to counter-attack. Attacks and counter-attacks probably contributed to the reasons for the divorce. If you could put yourself in either role, the attacker or the accused, how would you stop the argument? What responsibility should either parent take that may diffuse the blaming?

Did you notice the "you" statements in the examples? The "you" statements are an indictment requiring a defense. Like going to court, you now have an adversary interaction. If you listen carefully to your arguments, you will hear "you" statements or indictments. What are you to do? Try making "I" statements, talking more about yourself and your feelings in response to what the other person is saying instead of "you, you, you." Instead of saying, "*You* don't know anything about how to care for a two-year-old." Try saying, "*I* am very nervous about how you are going to care for Amy if she gets sick during the night. Could you tell me what you would do?" The "I" statement will get you a very different reaction from your ex-spouse. It takes practice to first learn to monitor your language and then plan on how to change "you" statements to "I" statements.

Tip: Avoid making "you" statements; instead use "I" statements.

When little Billy does something troubling or perhaps something that you don't expect after visiting his other parent, it's easy to assume that the unexplained change in the behavior is the other parent's fault. When feeling blamed, the first response is to deny responsibility rather than question your role in the problem. Denial is an emotional defense to protect our self-image as a competent and loving parent who wishes no harm to our children. Blaming is an offensive strategy that alienating parents use, and denial is a defensive strategy for the victim. This is part of the alienating cycle. Blaming and denial prevent change from happening. Instead, the animosity grows. When you are blamed, you have little choice but to defend yourself.

Tip: Blaming will cause a parent to feel victimized because he or she feels powerless to stop the attack.

When you notice your child has become distant, deflated, or unable to speak above a whisper or look you in the eye, your parental instincts kick into gear. You want to protect him, to help him, and to make everything better and prevent bad things from happening again. Unfortunately, you don't really know what has happened to cause a change in your child's behavior or attitude. Your natural inclination is to theorize the reasons for his feelings and behavior. Like most parents involved in high conflict with the ex-spouse, it is easy to blame the ex-spouse for your child's apparent sadness.

"Mommy said that you gave me head lice."

You will deny the allegation but still feel helpless in stopping the assault. You can be totally helpless because you cannot explain your child's behavior or attitude. Coming up with a plausible theory to explain your children's behavior may temporarily relieve that helpless feeling if you can blame someone. Your ex-spouse is an easy target, especially if he isn't around to defend himself. It is easy to say that the problem is all your ex-spouse's fault.

> Tip: Telling your child that something is your ex-spouse's fault is alienating. Instead, address the issue with the ex-spouse and do not put your child in the middle.

If you're still angry or disgusted with your ex-spouse for past behavior, you're primed to unequivocally believe your critical theories. It is consistent with what you previously believed about your ex-spouse. Blaming or targeting the other parent prevents you from feeling guilty or taking any responsibility for the situation. Unfortunately, taking yourself off the hook in this manner will ultimately intensify your frustration and add to your sense of powerlessness when the other parent fails to act to your satisfaction. The other risk is believing that your feelings validate your theory, otherwise, why would you feel the way you do. After all, if your ex-spouse is totally to blame for your children's unhappiness, only he or she can stop your children's pain; not you.

> Tip: Blaming others rather than taking personal responsibility can contribute to a parent's depression. Stop blaming and begin taking control over what you have the power to change.

> Tip: Having a feeling in response to your theory does not make the theory true. Because you feel your belief is right doesn't make it right or true. This is emotional reasoning.

Naturally, things can go wrong during parenting time. Sometimes in response children get a "zombie" look on their face when asked about what went wrong in the other household. This is a way that the child defends himself from an uncomfortable situation. You may even have good cause from past experiences for being suspicious, but you are still theorizing and reacting to a premise that could be anywhere from completely off-the-mark to being true. The reality of the situation is, you don't know.

Tip: You can't read minds. You can only ask for clarification.

To reduce misunderstandings and needless conflict, try to examine your feelings before taking an action. Take a moment to ask yourself, "Have I drawn a conclusion based on something I actually saw or heard or know to be true, and not merely something I think happened or believe could be true? Did I consider and eliminate other explanations to explain what happened before coming up with my own theory?"

Tip: Children also hypothesize and may misunderstand a parent's words or behavior. Do not expect your child to ask for clarification. They too will emotionally react as if their theory were true.

The only way any of us can ever really know the meaning of another person's actions is for that person to explain his or her behavior. However, people rarely volunteer that information, and we rarely ask. Instead you must ask for clarification rather than assume your theory is correct.

Nothing disrupts communication more than blaming the other parent for something. The notion that the other parent deliberately did something to hurt you is implied in the accusations. The blaming parent makes assumptions about the other parent's motivation, alleging, "I know you did that just to hurt me." Underlying blame is the parent making assumptions or theorizing about the other parent's motives. The indictment is sure to cause a fight and maybe a return to court. An effective way of avoiding a fight and making the other parent defensive is to reword your accusation from a declarative sentence to a question. Instead of saying, "I know you interfered with visits" say instead, "Did you interfere with visits?" You may get a very different reaction to your statement.

"I am tired of your disrespect. You never let me talk to Billy on the phone without you standing behind him, telling him what to say. I know you are trying to influence what Billy says to me."

"You don't know anything."
"Then let me ask, why don't you let Billy have some privacy when he is talking with me?"

We don't know how the parent would respond to the other parent's question. That would be hypothesizing. What we *can* assume is if the question is asked with sincerity, spoken calmly, with a willingness to listen without a counter-attack, the exchange may be very different. Maybe the parent will get an answer that offers some insight about how to give Billy more privacy. There are no guarantees, only hope for improvement. When trying new ways to communicate, do not expect immediate results, especially if there is a history of distrust. Also, you are less likely to see success with an obsessed parent.

No one likes being told what they are feeling. I am sure you have had the experience where someone is saying you feel such and such, and upon reflection you say to yourself, "No, I don't feel that way." Telling a person how they feel is blaming and offensive. This may be true even when hearing your therapist telling you how you feel. If you really want to know how the other person is feeling, ask rather than tell them. Asking the question instead of making a declarative statement goes a long way toward minimizing the risk of an argument. An example is: "I know you are angry because I see it on your face." Instead, you can ask, "Are you angry?" Changing your language will get you a very different reaction and perhaps more cooperation.

Your approach with an obsessed parent must take into account his or her difficulties to stop, think, and empathize with what you are trying to say. Your goal is to reduce the obsessed parent's defensiveness. It may be helpful to be patient and let them vent their rage without your getting defensive. Resist any attempt to counter-attack unless you want the fighting to escalate. I know this requires tremendous self-control and may not help. Again, you have to consider the odds of success, escalating the fighting or the possibility of getting to the point where the two of you can calmly talk to each other. Resist your temptation to blame. After the tensions subside, try calmly to discuss the issue, carefully avoiding any blame but instead stick to the single issue. You want to resist getting off track by recounting the damaging history. You know that you are having some success when the tone of the obsessed parent's voice is calmer.

"Could we talk about how we are going to schedule Billy's summer visits?"

"Billy doesn't want to be gone that long from me during the summer. If you really cared about Billy, you wouldn't ask him to spend six weeks with you this summer if you thought about Billy rather than yourself."

"That is not what Billy is telling me. He is looking forward to spending time with his cousins and going to the beach."

"What do you know? He has seen how you have treated me and now he is afraid of you."

"I am confident about my relationship with Billy. Can we stay on the issue? The court order allows me to have six weeks with Billy. How can we schedule the time and arrange for the exchange?"

Tip: If you do not want to offend anyone, ask them rather than tell them their motives for doing something.

Before automatically blaming or rushing to conclusions, consider the following:

- Learn to recognize when you start blaming or theorizing. This is done by monitoring your own words and thinking.
- Replace "you" statements with "I" statements.
- Don't tell people how they feel. Instead, ask how they feel.
- Remind yourself that your "explanation" is really an interpretation that could be wrong. Before you spring into action, check out your theory by asking for clarification.
- Ask for clarification from the person whose behavior you're trying to understand. The mere act of asking causes you to pause and reduces your chances of overreacting. It gets you to slow down, listen, and hopefully make a thoughtful, conscious decision about what to say next. This is a vast improvement over blindly following the trail of convoluted reasoning winding through your mind.
- Children also theorize and blame. Because of their immaturity, children may not be able to discriminate between a theory and reality. Be cautious about believing what your children tell you.

- When seeking clarification from children, you won't always get clear, concise answers. They rarely come right out and say, "I feel sad about Dad not living with us anymore" or "I was afraid that I'd hurt your feelings if I hugged and kissed Mom in front of you." Instead, they might tell you they felt "weird" or "icky" or simply are not interested in kissing. Sometimes they will tell you what they think you want to hear, rather than taking the risk of upsetting you by being honest.

You may notice, if you listen carefully to people argue, that they spend a lot of time trying to recreate what happened in the past. The rationale, if there is one, is the belief that if you agree with my account of past events, you can't help but agree with my argument; this is usually not successful. Instead, the frustration and anger grows. When the pressure in the speech intensifies, you are losing the argument. If the person suddenly agrees with you, be careful trusting what they say. They may be backing down because they are tired of fighting. Rather than blaming and arguing about what happened in the past, try to agree on the issue being discussed.

"I think we need to talk about how to pay for Billy's braces. What are your thoughts? Can you help pay for them?"

"I give you enough money. I shouldn't have to pay for the braces. You have spent my child support on yourself, not on Billy."

"I know you think I don't spend the child support on Billy. It costs a lot to keep this house going. Our disagreement about how I spend the child support is not the issue. You have agreed that Billy needs braces and I don't have enough money to make the payments. It will cost about one hundred dollars a month. I need your help."

"How can I justify giving you more money after you leased a new car and took Billy is Disney World?

"I don't want to argue with you. We agreed that Billy needs braces and I need fifty dollars a month to pay for the braces. Are you willing to help? This is not for me—it's for Billy."

Try to agree to focus on the issue at hand and on what both of you are going to do different in the future, rather than trying to recreate history. The parent in the last example did well avoiding the trap of getting defensive and arguing about how money was spent in the past. The one parent kept the other parent on the issue without getting defensive and attacking.

What you agree to do in the future is the issue, not what happened in the past. Learning to be future-focused is not easy, so be patient. The question to be agreed upon is "What are we going to do differently in the future for our child's best interest?" not "What did we do in the past that hurts?"

....

Tip: Trying to get both parents to agree on past events rarely, if ever, works to bring about mutual understanding.

....

6

Obstacles to Change: Theorizing

"I don't care what you say. I know what you are thinking."

People are naturally inquisitive. If you are like most people, you want to know what makes people tick and why they do what they do. If you don't understand the reasons for why someone is behaving in a particular way and there is no reasonable explanation, you will most likely come up with your own theory; we all do this. The problem that arises is our inclination to emotionally react to our theory as if that theory were true. In fact, our emotional reaction usually reinforces in our mind that the theory is correct. Otherwise, why do we feel the way that we do?

If you have ever been called to your supervisor's office, you will understand what is meant by emotionally reacting to your theory. Imagine passing your supervisor in the hallway and his saying "I am glad I ran into you. Please come to my office at one o'clock." If you are like most people, you will question "What have I done wrong?" You will do a mental inventory of your past wrongdoings, and we can always find a past wrongdoing, because none of us are perfect. Now you are feeling nervous, reacting to your theory as if your theory were true. When you go to your supervisor's office, you may learn that his request to see you has nothing to do with your theory. You worried over nothing. I suspect that you can think of many examples from your past when you were worried about something and later learned that it was nothing at all as you had expected.

If you had a stormy marriage or a hostile divorce, you will be predisposed to interpret your ex-spouse's behavior in a negative light. You may be quick to judge and prone to misunderstand or theorize the reasons for the other's behavior. This is because you're looking at your ex-spouse's actions or comments through a lens clouded by pain, anger, bitterness, and memories of past experiences. In turn, theorizing intensifies your animosity toward your former partner. Your biased misinterpretation of your former partner's behavior may stem from a sincere desire to protect your children from an imaginary harm to their health and happiness. Jessie expressed her fear that "it is only a matter of time until John will abuse our daughter like he abused me," knowing that John has never threatened their daughter. Jessie is sincere about not wanting to see any harm come to their daughter, but her fear is intensified because of her theory and images that are conjured up in her imagination.

There is a risk that will make matters worse; that risk is the parent conveying her fears to her daughter. A parent's fears can be conveyed to the child verbally or with subtle facial expressions or gestures. This is an example of alienation. The child may not understand what is being said or the meaning of the parent's gestures. Now the child has no other choice but to hypothesize about the meaning of the parent's comments or expressions. The child in this example can learn to unfairly fear the targeted parent. Keep in mind that most children will not have the maturity or forethought to ask for clarification. Children want to believe that their mother or father always tells the truth, even if the children are told an untruth.

Ron and Susan

Divorced parents in their mid-thirties, Ron and Susan had initially managed to keep conflicts over parenting to a minimum. A little over a year after their break-up, Susan, the custodial parent, ran into her ex-husband while shopping in the mall with nine-year-old Brett and seven-year-old Mary. She glanced at Brett and Mary to see how they reacted to seeing their father. Instead of rushing over to hug him as she'd expected, both wore blank expressions on their faces and stood several feet away from him, looking listless. The children's reactions confused her. From Susan's perspective, they appeared scared to approach Ron. She theorized that something was terribly wrong. "What has he done to make them afraid of him?" she wondered. "If he's hurt them in any way, I'll kill him." She could barely resist the urge to grab their hands and rush away.

Ron also noticed how emotionally withdrawn his children appeared, but he had a different theory explaining their demeanor. "They're clearly unhappy with their mother," he concluded. "She must be making their lives miserable like she did with me." He was angry and wanted to wrench his children away from Susan on the spot. Neither Ron nor Susan acted on their impulses, but the damage was done.

Reacting to their respective theories each felt protective of the children and became increasingly suspicious of the other. They grilled their kids about what went on when they were with the other parent and were constantly on the look-out for signs of abuse and neglect. At one point, Ron even considered seeking custody of his children and Susan thought about cutting off visitation. This all came about because of what turned out to be invalid theories about why the children behaved as they did.

"Mommy says that I need to be afraid and worried when I go to Daddy's house."

Brett and Mary didn't feel afraid or unhappy, but rather awkward and unsure about how to handle an unfamiliar situation (running into Dad at the mall while they were with Mom). If they had rushed over to greet their father, they might've hurt their mother's feelings. But if they stayed right next to their mother, their father might feel rejected. They resolved their dilemma as many children would have, which was by physically and emotionally distancing themselves.

Brett and Mary withdrew physically and emotionally by stepping away from their mother, avoiding eye contact, and taking on the most noncommittal look they could muster; a blank, almost trance-like expression. They didn't need rescuing or protection, but reassurance and direction from their mother. If either parent understood how the children felt, or if Susan had reserved judgment and simply mentioned to her kids that they were welcome to go over and say "Hi" to their dad, months of wrangling between the parents would have been avoided. Sometimes, we parents must remember that children don't think like us and instead need guidance and sometimes permission about how to act in a strange and unique situation. This is an opportunity to mentor the children. We should not expect children to act like adults and ask, "Mom, what should I do when I see you and Dad together?" This question isn't likely to be asked.

Tip: Children avoid what makes them uncomfortable. The avoidance can be that blank look on their faces or answering a simple question saying, "I don't know."

Trying to physically or emotionally avoid the tension the way Brett and Mary did, is a typical childhood reaction. Youngsters will use it when they get caught sneaking cookies from the pantry, have to endure Aunt Jane's cheek-pinching at a family gathering, or are torn between pleasing their teacher by telling her who hid the chalkboard erasers and being loyal to a friend by not telling. It's a mainstay escape mechanism among children whose divorced parents have trouble getting along.

As I've said, arguments and icy silences between their parents upset children. Tense situations that come with the territory of divorce confuse them. Just saying good-bye after a visit can pose a dilemma for the children, especially if they believe the parents are watching from the doorway or from the living room window. How affectionate can their parting be without hurting you? How enthusiastically can they greet you without hurting their other parent? Your theorizing and reacting to your irrational beliefs don't make matters better.

These awkward situations are just too complicated for their childlike psyches to handle, so they tune out their surroundings, turn off their feelings, and get that familiar blank expression on their faces. Because younger children don't know how to explain their feelings, they withdraw while older teens instead deny being bothered. Sometimes, without being conscious of their motives, they let out their feelings in some other venue. They may fight in the playground, complain of stomach pains requiring special attention from the school nurse, or find other ways of seeking attention. Unfortunately, parents don't always realize that a simple desire to avoid unpleasantness or escape discomfort is behind the blank looks on their children's faces and the almost depressed quality to their appearances.

Theorizing is probably a good example of the crux of how irrational beliefs can influence irrational feelings. Irrational beliefs are not founded in reality and lead to irrational behavior. During our daily activities, we are constantly making judgments about events. For the most part, we are able to respond appropriately to our environment because we understand the events around us. The interpretation of an event does not have to be negative or threatening if we have sufficient self-esteem or confidence in being able to cope with the situation. On the other hand, a person could misinterpret an event in a way that is threatening if the individual is insecure or feels threatened. Controlling the anxiety and avoiding irrational behavior begins by first learning to recognize when you are theorizing. This requires you to monitor your behavior and be honest with yourself when you do not understand something. Learn to catch yourself when you are theorizing about someone else's motives. Then ask questions to clarify your concerns to the person who has the answers. Asking questions of your ex-spouse can be uncomfortable but if you preface the question with your desire to understand, your ex-spouse may feel less threatened and give you a reasonable answer. Remember, your ex-spouse will also theorize and may inappropriately react to your statements or behavior. Theorizing works both ways.

Tip: Ask questions of the person who has the answers rather than theorizing. This will help prevent excessive anxiety and irrational behavior.

Theorizing is anticipating future events, rather than present reality. Almost everyone has had the experience of feeling fearful of an anticipated event and then later, after experiencing the event, finding that there was no reason to worry. Your anxiety will subside when you replace theory with reality. With answers to your questions, you are more likely to know how to act appropriately rather than making erroneous conclusions and provoking irrational emotional reactions. Asking questions rather than making assumptions will help prevent alienations and excessive stress to your children. Learning to stop theorizing takes practice and is not easy to accomplish. You have a lot to gain in all aspects of your life when you learn these skills.

Setting the Stage for Reunification

"How can I expect to see my children when their father sabotages me at every turn?"

Angry parents enter the court ready to attack and expect to defend their arguments in typical adversarial thinking. You may think your story is unique, believing that the judge cannot help but agree with your arguments. However, the judge has heard your story many times over and may have little interest in who is right and who is wrong. Blaming does not help the children. The court focuses on making a decision that appears fair, lessens the conflicts between the parties, and ultimately protects the children. The judge will assess your arguments against how the state judges best interest. The difficulty is your not knowing how much weight the judge will place on the different criteria. The judge may agree that alienation has occurred but place less weight on that argument than on other criteria. When the court order cannot fix the problems between parents and the children and there are doubts that the parents can work out their differences, reunification therapy is an option.

Tip: Proving alienation may not be enough to win custody.

The process to reunification consists of a team of professionals defined by the court: a guardian *ad litem*, a parent coordinator, a visitation center staff member, a reunification therapist, or anyone else who the court believes should be involved. The court usually decides the composition of the team with the attorneys' agreement.

There is a distinction between what is referred to as reunification and reunification therapy (RT). Reunification therapy occurs between the therapist and the family. The focus is threefold: tempering the hostilities of the alienating parent, assuring an emotional and safe environment for the children with both parents and significant others, and repairing the damaged relationships with the children. The term *reunification therapy* is becoming more common, though detailed treatment protocols for reunification therapy are minimal.

Reunification therapy is a recent modality for treating high-conflict litigious families. Reunification emphasizes case management (Sullivan and Kelly 2001; Barris, Coats, Duvall, Garrity, Johnson, and LaCrosse 2001) using court-appointed mediators, parent coordinators, or special masters to monitor compliance with court orders and educate the parents about working together. Though these approaches are effective for most high-conflict families, they are less effective with the severely alienated child and the obsessed parent. Reunification alone does not address the unique problems with these parents and children who refuse any cooperation with the targeted parent.

Reunification therapy remains a difficult task because the alienating parent and child usually have little or no desire to participate in the therapy. They may try to sabotage any gains made with the children, miss appointments, and discount any value from the therapy. This can be a good argument for removing the children from the alienating parent if the pattern of behavior persists with the alienating parent during the reunification process.

Forcing or coercing alienating parents with threats if they do not change their behavior may work for a short time, but not for the long term. Lasting change will only occur when change happens with the parent's belief system or with behavior that does not hinder the child's relationship with the targeted parent. Change for the severely alienated child presents more difficulty because young children typically do not respond well to traditional talk therapy. Treatment to lessen the children's anxiety against the targeted parent may be more effective.

Frequently courts and attorneys are frustrated with high-conflict families because of repeated trips to court, failure to follow court orders, and continued hostilities that risk damaging the children. High-conflict cases never seem to be resolved especially if the case involved a parent obsessed with destroying the relationship between the children and the targeted parent. The parents may even attack their attorney's and the therapist's ethics. Courts search for answers, often looking to the mental health community for therapists experienced with helping to heal parent-child relationships.

Recent trends seek alternatives to the traditional judicial system for helping divorce couples to work together. One model is the collaborative divorce (Tesler and Thompson, 2006) that focuses on training professionals, usually attorneys, about using the model to reduce "collateral damage" to the families and to simplify the divorce process for parents. The model has opponents who argue that the attorney's ethical commitment must advocate for their client's interest. The American Bar Association (Hoffman 2007) ". . . affirms that lawyers do not need to be gladiators in order to satisfy fully their ethical duty to represent clients diligently. Rather, it is entirely ethical for lawyers to work solely toward an out-of-court settlement that is acceptable to the clients."

Courts order family or individual therapy to supplement case management. Courts rarely use the term reunification therapy in the court order, partly because they rarely know who in the community is qualified to provide the unique therapy. Very often, courts leave the selection of the therapist to the attorneys with the parents' approval.

Tip: Do not expect special treatment in court.

No consensus exists about how to define successful reunification. Successful reunification implies more than a successful reconnection between a rejected parent and the estranged or alienated child. Reunification must include the child having a reciprocal and safe relationship with *both* parents. Some mental health professionals may disagree because of the concern that the alienating parent is emotionally abusive and manipulative. They will argue that a more realistic goal involves helping the child reconnect with the targeted parent and undo the negative programming by the alienating parent. The goal implies that the alienating parent may not change, and that certainly can be true. Success may include limited contact with the alienating parent. However, there is concern about who should define the circumstances for denying a parent access to his or her child. Assuming that the child's safety is not an issue, the decision to deny access should occur after attempts to reunify have failed and the likelihood of continued alienation persists. This is especially important if false allegations of abuse continue. Noncompliance to court orders also represents failure.

Children should not feel caught in the middle; they should never have to choose one parent over the other. Courts and state legislators are starting to recognize the harm caused by having children choose one parent over the other. True, the children's feelings should be considered but that is not the deciding criteria. Court's will typically put more weight on what an older child says than on what a younger child says. Child advocates may argue that children should have the right to choose, but for the alienated child, the consequences are too severe since the child's judgment is questionable. The child's public pronouncement of choosing a parent becomes the ultimate rejection and is difficult for the child to take back. For these reasons, many states have eliminated the age of election, meaning the age a child is able to choose where to live. Instead, most states have a provision for the child to express his or her wishes but the decision still rests with the court and what is considered to be in the child's best interest. Reunification is not choosing the rejected parent over the alienating one. However, both parents must respect the child's dignity and right to have a reciprocal relationship with both parents, free of interference and exposure to further alienating or estranging behaviors from either parent.

Controlling Volatile Issues

Reunification or working to resolve conflicts between you and the ex-spouse requires both parents to maintain self-control over their anger or hurt. You must resist any temptation to retaliate with your own alienating behavior. Do not do anything that causes your attorney to have to defend your behavior. False allegations of poor parenting are bad enough; do not add to the problem by legitimizing your ex-spouse's complaints. Doing so can severely weaken your case.

> *Tip: Do not impulsively make verbal threats to your ex-spouse unless you want to make matters worse.*

Always remain calm when confronting an emotionally charged matter. When you two start to argue and your voices get loud, take a time out. Announce your intention to cool off, then walk away, or allow the other person to withdraw. Try again when you both have your anger under control. You may need a third party or a therapist to help you both to maintain control.

> *Tip: Losing control of your anger never strengthens a relationship. You only instill fear and anxiety.*

When someone's speech becomes loud and pressured, your chances of getting through to that person or resolving a problem are nil. You can't "win" or even get your message across because the other person is not listening to what you have to say. Instead of pursuing this futile endeavor, acknowledge that the discussion has obviously stirred up some strong feelings and suggest that you both back off for a while. Agree to discuss the issue at another time.

Tip: Do not attempt to resolve differences between you and your ex-spouse when either of you has pressured speech. Setting the stage for reunification requires both of you to remain calm.

During the therapy you must maintain self-control. Getting overtly angry with your ex-spouse or the therapist will not help your cause. If need be, ask your therapist if you can walk out and calm down, understanding that you will return in a few minutes. Do not leave and not go back.

Accessing Your Children

A parent cannot hope for reunification or rebuilding a relationship with their child if they have no access to the child. Waiting for time to pass, hoping the child will spontaneously say "I now want to see my father" doesn't happen. If you cannot spend time with your children, you cannot prevent further damage or provide hope to repair the damaged relationship with your children. Having access to your children is imperative. If you are not already seeing your child, you need a court order to see your children. With your attorney's guidance, be sure the court continues to support your parenting time with minimal supervision. Allegations of abuse or threats to the children's safety are the only good reasons for limiting your parenting time or requiring supervised visits. If you must abide with supervised visits, do so rather than losing all your time with the children. Even if you are angry, humiliated, or embarrassed by the restricted court order, you stand a better chance of continuing or rebuilding your parent-child relationship if you comply with the order. Do not let your pride get between you and your children.

If your ex-spouse has falsely accused you of child abuse, you must cooperate with the investigation and try insisting on supervised visits rather than no visits. Follow your attorney's instructions. Do not stop picking up your children for your scheduled parenting time. If the other parent refuses, keep showing up unless the court order says otherwise. If your ex-spouse refuses to cooperate with scheduled visits, keep a log of your attempts. Interference with scheduled visits can be painful and maddening, but stay calm when driving away. Do not make a scene. Your children may be watching from "behind the curtains." The alienating parent's failure to comply with court orders will support your legal pleadings to the court and force the alienating parent to defend his or her actions. Judges become offended when parents disobey court orders. If the court disagrees with the alienating parent's actions, the alienating parent could face "contempt of court" charges. Some judges use their punitive powers, ordering jail time, a monetary fine, or other sanctions to emphasize their expectations that court orders will be followed.

Irrational Belief: The relationship between the child and the targeted parent will improve by doing nothing.

Supervised Visits

Courts will order supervised visits when there is a concern about the children's emotional or physical safety or reasons to believe that the children are afraid of the rejected parent. Sometimes, the court's decision for supervised visits is because of false information provided by the alienating parent. The risk of ordering supervised visits is the subtle message to the child that the targeted parent is a threat to the child's safety. The threat can be reinforced by the alienating parent's comments like, "Honey, don't worry, the nice lady at the center will protect you."

Supervised visits should only occur in conjunction with reunification therapy or some court-ordered intervention to repair the damaged relationship. Supervised visits simply mean that the court has designated someone to observe the parent and children during limited visits. Supervised visits limit what you can do with your child. Your visit could be limited to one room or the center's backyard, rather than attending a special activity or sharing a relaxed day at home. Restricted access helps ensure the child's safety but limits your ability to heal the relationship. Because of the visitation center's rules, both of you can feel inhibited. You may not be able to hug or exchange gifts. A theory behind supervised visits is giving you additional time to regain your child's trust and to become more relaxed.

Tip: Court-ordered supervised visits must define, in the court order, under what conditions the supervised visits should be reduced or eliminated.

The alienating parent may not share in this goal. I remember a mother described how her son warmed up to his father during a supervised visit and together they had a great time. In response, the mother grabbed her son's hand, ran out of the visitation center never to be seen again. This mother was not interested in her son having an affectionate or fun relationship with his father. The mother's agenda was clearly more important than what was best for her son. The person supervising and observing the visits will report any progress or problems to the court.

When a court orders supervised visits the court typically is silent about many important questions, such as:

- What criteria does the court use to extend or eliminate supervised visits? The criteria should be an improvement in the parent-child relationship rather than a calendar date.

- Who makes the decision to extend parenting time? Using the therapist as a gatekeeper causes ethical problems and should be avoided. There should be an impartial person capable of making this decision without having to wait to return to court. Serious delays in busy jurisdictions hurt the parent-child relationship, cause frustration, and become very expensive for the parents. A special master, guardian *ad litem* or parent coordinator may serve in a limited role as arbitrator who is able to make these decisions.

- What reparative or corrective actions does the court order to promote an improved relationship? Typically, visitation centers do not allow the two parents to see or talk with each other for fear that their hostilities will get out of control. The concern is realistic but does not help with the parents' learning to work together. In effect, the typical protocol used by many visitation centers does little to repair parent resentments.

The court should not assign the therapist supervisory responsibilities. In many jurisdictions, doing so is unethical and places the therapist in an awkward position of being the gatekeeper. The therapist becomes the object of the parents' manipulations, which detracts from therapy. Attorneys should advocate against well-meaning court orders that give the therapist authority to modify parenting time. A parent coordinator, or some impartial individual assigned by the court to monitor progress, should make decisions or offer recommendations to the court to modify access. The parent coordinator would consult with the therapist before making the decision. If the court grants the parent coordinator limited arbitration power to make quicker decisions and changes in scheduled time, families will save considerable money.

Courts have ordered the supervised visits to occur at the custodial parent's home, having the custodial parent serve as the supervisor. The rationale is that the child will be most comfortable in that setting. This may not be true. One parent expected to supervise said, "I hate it when I have to supervise the visit because Jim wants to talk to me about the divorce rather than spending time with his son. I resent being manipulated." This mother made a good point. If you are required to have supervised visits at the custodial parent's home, focus on spending positive time with your children, and be polite but ignore your ex-spouse. Do not expect to talk with your ex-spouse about the divorce or the court proceedings. This advice is also true for the supervising parent. Your children should not be in a position where they can overhear your discussions about the proceedings. Forcing these discussions where the children can hear is alienating and raises the children's fears.

Tip: Do not discuss court-related issues where your children can hear.

During these trying times, keep a log of your activities for your attorney. When you have time with the children, focus on keeping your relationship positive. Compliment them, show interest in their activities, and listen to what they say. Your child must feel good about you to prevent PAS. Do not pump your children for information, criticize or denigrate the other parent, or push for physical affection. Let your child set the pace. Otherwise, you may be doing what you criticize the other parent for doing. Your best defense against alienation is strengthening the relationship and the bond with your child. Keep your attorney informed of any problems you encounter.

Tip: Parents frequently ask, "How do I know my decision about what to do is the right decision?" The answer typically is, "What will reduce your child's anxiety with you?" That is usually the best answer. Your child's reaction to what you decide also says whether your decision was correct. Does your child smile and continue to be spontaneous or do they go blank on you?

Criteria for Success

Judging successful reunification occurs in two ways. The court's perspective of success may be different from the parent's perspective, though they should share some common goals. The court's goals for successful reunification are:

- To never return to court with the same legal arguments.
- Comply with court-ordered parenting time.
- Stop the hurt by the parents and children, learning better control of their anger and bitterness.

- Stop denigrating (alienating) behavior.
- Facilitate a reciprocal loving relationship between the children, both parents, and extended family.
- Repair any damage done to the child's relationship with the alienated parent.

The criteria for successful reunification are different for the alienated child, the alienating parent, and targeted parent. Successful intervention for the alienated child should include but not be limited to:

- Feeling safe and trusting that basic emotional and physical needs are met.
- Any opinions expressed by the child toward a parent are grounded on reality and personal experience, rather than from either parent's delusional or distorted beliefs.
- Showing affection appropriately toward both parents without the fear of hurting the other parent.
- Having continued access to both parents and extended family now and in the future.

For the alienating parent to:

- Reduce alienating behavior toward the targeted parent and with the children.
- Assure that the relationship with the children remains strong for years to come.
- Learn appropriate communication to strengthen his or her relationship with the children while reducing conflict with the other parent.
- Find ways to repair the damage that alienation has caused the children.
- Not interfere with the targeted parent's reasonable or court-ordered access to the children.

For the targeted parent to:

- Enjoy unimpeded parenting time with the children.
- Heal the suffering caused by previous alienation.
- Learn ways to reduce conflict and alienating behavior.

For both parents to:

- Eliminate hurtful comments about each other.
- Develop empathy with the children.
- Improve the relationship between the children and the extended family.
- Communicate calmly and make joint decisions.

Accomplishing these goals is difficult, particularly because not everyone is motivated to change. The other parent may see their interest best served by doing nothing. Some parents argue that they are not alienating because they do nothing, remaining passive. What these parents do not understand is that their passivity can actually reinforce alienation, such as letting the child choose whether to visit the other parent or not correcting their child when they cuss out the other parent.

Therapy and education work well with naive and active alienators but is not as effective in helping an obsessed alienator. Obsessed parents get very defensive when their beliefs are questioned. Confrontation only further entrenches their irrational beliefs, giving them reason to drop out of therapy. The therapist must create a comfortable milieu to get past the defenses. Obsessed parents will ignore court orders and drop out of therapy, believing that they are somehow protecting the child.

Outcome Studies

There are no studies supporting the efficacy of different treatment interventions with high-conflict parents and reunification. Richard Gardner, M.D. (2001) conducted a follow-up study comparing the outcomes of ninety-nine cases in which he consulted about issues of parental alienation syndrome. In twenty-two cases, the court followed his recommendation, forcing visitation or transfer of custody. In seventy-seven cases, the court chose to ignore his recommendations. Gardner acknowledged that he did not conduct follow-up telephone interviews with the identified alienating parent, leaving in doubt the child's relationship with that parent after the court action. He reasoned, "I did not call alienating parents because I suspect (and I believe with justification) that they would not be fully cooperative with me with regard to providing accurate information." Gardner's reasons may be correct but this argues for an independent study. Gardner's study implied that successful reunification does not have to include a positive relationship with both parents. I do not consider exchanging one parent's involvement with a child at the detriment of the other parent successful reunification. Some may argue that improving the relationship with the targeted parent without knowing what happened to the relationship with the alienating parent is still a degree of success. In some situations that may be true, but before giving up on the alienating parent, both parents should be given the opportunity to learn to work together.

Dunne and Hedrich (1994) and Lampel (1986) found similar limitations for defining successful intervention for alienated parents. Questionable criteria for successful reunification do not necessarily invalidate the conclusions of their studies that a transfer of custody or limiting the child's access to the alienating parent, rather than providing traditional psychotherapy, may be more effective in stemming alienation. If the criterion for successful reunification is to include the child's opportunity for a reciprocal positive relationship with both parents, the methodology used for outcome studies must include verification from both parents. There needs to be outcome studies documenting the efficacy of any treatment approaches, including what is proposed in this book. This will be very difficult because getting an adequate sample size and developing a controlled study is next to impossible.

Courts frequently order the child into counseling when the child refuses to have any contact with the rejected parent. Though the court order may make sense, the order can have serious negative repercussions to the child. The judge or magistrate wants to protect and not risk harming the child. Although a common practice, it gives the child a subtle message that the problems in the family are his or her fault. The child may feel responsible to fix the problems between the parents. This is a very irrational burden to put on a child. For many children, counseling makes them feel bored or uncomfortable. The child may blame the rejected parent for forcing them into counseling. A better alternative is to order both parents, and not the children, to counseling. The therapist should have access to the children when needed in the therapist's judgment.

Sometimes, therapy for the child is appropriate if the child is suffering from a serious mental disorder. If the reunification therapist finds the child's general functioning is impaired for whatever reason, a different therapist may need to intervene. Impaired functioning is a drop in school grades, evidence of depression, impaired social relationships, or belligerent behavior, etc. If the child already sees a therapist, he or she should continue. The child's therapist should know that the family is participating in reunification therapy.

Professionals in psychology and law are now developing protocols for reunification. Reunification therapy is different from traditional therapy in many ways. A consensus in the literature describes the differences:

- Reunification must be court-ordered to help assure compliance and to identify the participants. An order also identifies who is responsible to pay for services.

- Because the therapy is court-ordered, insurance usually does not pay for the treatment. Expect to pay out of pocket.

- The reunification therapist cannot be the same individual who conducted the court-ordered evaluation. Nor should the therapist have a prior professional relationship with any of the parties. This is a dual relationship that is considered an ethical violation (American Psychological Association 2002) and may lead to a sanction by the therapist's state licensing board. All parties should agree on the selection of the therapist. Parents should not expect the therapist to make a custody or visitation recommendation to the court. The court should assign someone neutral to monitor the parents' compliance to the court order and make recommendations to the court. The monitor can be a guardian *ad litem*, special master, or parent coordinator. The monitor should not be the therapist, mediator, or an attorney for either party.

- Typically, but not always, parents are more likely to comply with court orders if they know their behavior and compliance to court orders are monitored. Parents obsessed with their desire to alienate may ignore court orders, believing that no one is going to tell them what to do. They believe they must protect the children at all cost. They argue that the court does not understand the risks involved with the child having a relationship with the rejected parent. Courts expect parents to explain the reasons for their refusal to cooperate. The parent may have to defend their reasons why they should not be sanctioned. Parents risk sanctions if the court believes the parent's arguments make no sense, serve only to flagrantly disregard the court's power, or if the parent's actions were especially outrageous. The court may give a parent a second chance. Targeted parents are angry when they see the alienating parent gets only a slap on the hand for noncompliance. Unfortunately, after a couple slaps on the hand, the alienating parent's arrogance and defiance is reinforced. Sometimes the alienated parent will flaunt (in the targeted parent's face) the court's refusal to sanction, making matters worse.

- The therapist must have the flexibility to work with all parties and exchange information without being hampered by confidentiality. The therapist cannot have an allegiance to one parent or child to the detriment of the others. Prior to initiating reunification therapy, the therapist will ask the parents to sign an informed consent form explaining the therapy guidelines, granting a waiver of confidentiality, and assigning responsibility for fees. During reunification therapy, no protection of confidentiality will exist between all parties (parents, children, judge or other court-appointed persons, and all therapists). Protecting a parent's past medical or mental health records is the exception. These records remain confidential.

- The therapist needs the authority to determine the number and frequency of sessions and participants.

- The "family relationships," rather than specific family members, are the identified "client." Because the family and family relationships are the identified "client," insurance companies may not pay for sessions. Insurance billing requires an identified patient with a valid mental health diagnosis. An ethical therapist will not risk his or her license to lie on an insurance form. That is fraud. Another consideration: do you want a false mental health diagnosis attached to your name under these circumstances? That diagnosis could be later disclosed to the court and used against you.

- During reunification therapy, the therapists may identify issues with either parent or child that warrant a referral for traditional therapy. A referral and involvement of another therapist must occur so the reunification therapist avoids an ethical conflict or dual relationship. Insurance companies will more likely pay for traditional therapy if the reunification therapist makes a referral and there is a valid diagnosis for the patient receiving the therapy. Parents should clearly separate the two therapies in their thinking.

- Expect the therapist to be direct with his or her recommendations about how to behave in different circumstances.

- A new spouse or a grandparent can destroy any progress parents and children make in their therapy. The alienating parent's source of support (spouse and extended family) may need to participate in the therapy and be educated about their contribution to the problem. The therapist needs the ability to see anyone who may play a role in the alienation.

Tip: Do not expect the reunification therapist to testify and make custody or parenting time recommendations.

Other methods proposed for breaking the stalemate include an involuntary change of custody to the targeted parent or threatening to put an alienating or noncompliant parent in jail. This creates a crisis in the alienating parent's mind and can break a stalemate. This approach may not change a parent's attitude, but there are anecdotal reports that a crisis will get an oppositional parent to cooperate with court orders and this allows the targeted parent to resume parenting time. Creating a crisis should occur in conjunction with reunification therapy.

Do not expect a therapist to track down an uncooperative parent; this is not the therapist's responsibility. If the other parent refuses to cooperate, the therapist will notify the court or the referral source. Do not worry if you find yourself alone in therapy. The court will learn about your cooperation and the other parent's refusal to cooperate. The other parent's attorney will have to defend his or her client's refusal to comply with the court orders.

Tip: Do not try to influence the therapist behind the other parent's back. You will only be hurting yourself.

Preparing for reunification is not easy. You may be fraught with many emotions: anxiety, eagerness, renewed hope, or pessimism. Do not push the therapist because you are eager to resume an active relationship with your children. You must be patient and receptive to the idea that you, as well as your ex-spouse, will be making some changes. If you cannot accept that idea, then both you and your child lose.

Parent/Child Reunification Therapy

"What can I do? My children hate me."

This is perhaps the most complex issue facing an alienated parent. How do I fix my relationship with my child when he says he hates me? The rejected parent and the court's most immediate answer is to get the child into therapy. Without the alienating parent's cooperation and belief that the child's best interests are served with reunification, this rarely works. There is always the risk that the alienating parent will sabotage any progress toward reunification. This is usually the argument for changing custody to the targeted parent. A parent obsessed in destroying the relationship will see no self-interest in reunification. So what should the rejected parent do?

The Child's Perspective

Sometimes the children are the silent victims of the divorce. How well they communicate their feelings depends on their age, language skills, and psychological safety. It is easy for a parent to believe that the children are adjusting well when they do not speak. The parent looks to the child's behavior as a gauge of the child's adjustment. Acting out, a depressed mood, and withdrawal from friends are all reasons to be concerned.

The worse fear for a parent is to hear, "I don't want to see you ever again." After hearing the contempt in your child's voice and recovering from the shock of disbelief, you can feel the wrenching pain in your heart. You have nowhere to turn. You know you cannot shake your child back to reality. With all the talk about parental alienation syndrome over the past years, there are still no validated treatment protocols to reverse the damage caused by the overzealous parent. There continues to be speculation about the effectiveness of changing the alienated child's custody to the targeted parent. Then there is the notion of referring the child to therapy, frequently reinforcing in the child's mind that he or she is at fault or at least that he or she is responsible for maneuvering his or her life between two warring parents. With a little forethought, it is easy to see that such a recommendation is absurd and rarely works. The focus of the therapy has to be with both parents, having the children available to the reunification therapist.

> Tip: The parents and not the child should be the identified patient
> for reunification therapy.

Children may not share their feelings, but they are listening and watching their parents' behavior for any cue about how Mom or Dad is feeling. Sometimes parents respond to their hurt and anger by shutting down their emotions and distancing themselves from the children. They do so thinking they are protecting the children or perhaps because they are severely depressed and lack energy to face these issues with the children. They put on a brave face trying to assure the children that everything will be okay. This is certainly understandable. However, shutting down may be interpreted by the children as not caring. This is a dilemma for the children. On one hand, they want their parents to share their feelings and offer reassurance but on the other hand, they do not want to incite the parent's bitterness or sadness. Children do not want to cause their parents to cry or feel sad. Many do not want to be their parent's sounding board as they browbeat the other parent.

> Tip: Do not expect your child to be a sounding board, talking about
> adult issues that are not their business. You are blurring your role as
> the parent.

The approach the therapist uses to change the child's behaviors and beliefs has to take into consideration the child's age and developmental level. Younger children are less likely to respond to the cognitive approaches to change. The cognitive approaches such as reframing, self-monitoring, and soliciting feedback may not work well with younger children but may be more effective with teenagers who display some motivation to participate in the therapy. Desensitization, role-playing, and support will probably be more effective with the younger children. The goal for younger children is to reduce their anxiety toward the targeted parent and reframe their belief from hate to having nothing to fear from the targeted parent.

Tip: A treatment goal for the alienated child is to reduce the child's anxiety toward the targeted parent.

Communicating with children can be difficult because they can give the therapist or the parent the impression they understand and agree with what is said when, in fact, they do not understand. Children will misunderstand, like adults. Children usually want to please, or if they are very resistant and do not listen, they may give the false impression that they agree. When children do not understand, the therapist may have more success if he or she uses creative metaphors. Children respond very well to metaphors because the metaphor creates a psychological distance that makes it safer for the child to understand. An example is describing to the young child how a lion cub feels safer with both parents protecting him instead of saying Mom and Dad both need to protect you.

Children victimized by parental alienation and showing symptoms of parental alienation syndrome can be particularly difficult to work with. Typically, they are more motivated to fight therapy than cooperate. They are very suspicious if they believe the therapist is aligned with the targeted parent. The therapist must remain neutral and not try to defend a parent or argue with the child. Frequently, they will put up a wall of silence, refusing to talk or offer any in-depth insight about why they feel the way they do. They frequently answer questions with "I don't know." Or they might offer an answer equally vague. They may just stare at the floor and avoid eye contact. The tone of their voice can be very soft and their answers to questions evasive. Play therapy can be an effective bridge to help the resistant child talk. Another approach to reduce their resistance is using a therapy dog. Children and adults alike melt with a loving therapy dog.

A withdrawn child frequently feels a lot of anxiety in approaching the subject of their targeted parent. Their desire to avoid is very strong and they will frequently feel trapped by having to participate in the therapy. It is important for these children to receive frequent reminders that they are there because of the court order, not because their mother or father requires their participation. The therapist needs to pay particular attention in building a relationship with this child. The therapist has to establish trust. The therapist should not in any way deceive the child or give the child the impression that they are being pressured to reunify. The therapist will have more success with a resistant child if he or she establishes a rapport and trust with the alienating parent. The premise is for the child to follow the parent's lead toward reunification. In addition, there always has to be concern that, whatever therapeutic gains, the alienating parent does not sabotage the gains when not in earshot of the therapist. The targeted parent frequently expresses this fear. If the therapist is unsuccessful in gaining the alleged alienating parent's participation after a time in therapy, the therapist may have to share these concerns with the court. The court may have to consider a temporary change of custody or have the children stay with a neutral family member during the reunification therapy. The alienating parent needs to understand that this is a possible consequence if the therapist believes the alienating parent is destroying any gains.

There are other children who may be enthusiastic about wanting to share their anger with the therapist. They can't wait to tell their story. They will give the therapist a litany of reasons for their hate. These children are very vocal, insisting that they want nothing to do with the target parent. Frequently, the reasons are irrational and not based upon their personal experience but instead on things told to them by others. These children are truly the victims of parental alienation syndrome.

Tip: Do not lie to your child to get them to the therapist.

Some parents fear that their child will have a fit when they learn they have to see a therapist. To avoid a confrontation, the parent lies to the child about where they are going. The parent's deception says something to the therapist about the parent's parenting and ability to control the child. After such an incident, the child has reason to distrust the parent. The parent should not lie—deal with the child's anger or resistance and let the therapist address the child's anger about coming to the therapy.

Children exposed to their warring parents rightfully complain that they feel very little control about what is happening to them. They may not verbalize their struggle with not knowing the truth about what they are told, how to appease each parent, and how to avoid having to take a side. This is true even when they are talking with a therapist. Rather than getting defensive or trying to convince your child that you are the honest and truthful parent, suggest to your child that you are confident in their making up their own mind from their personal experiences rather than what they are told by others. It is important to remember that children victimized by alienation will rarely agree with the alienated or targeted parent's account of past events because they are so well brainwashed that they parrot the alienating parent. Trying to convince the child that your perspective is the right perspective will only push your child further away. They will only begin opening up if they feel psychologically safe to talk without retribution or criticism.

Tip: Do not expect your child to agree with you about memories of past events. Their memories and interpretation of past events will be different from yours.

Advice to Parents

Parents must take time to understand their child's perspective of the divorce. One child expressed his feelings well, saying, "That it is not as much that we are stuck in the middle of the divorce, it is that the divorce has an affect on our parents. Like how they act. That is what is having the affect on us. My mom makes a lot more mistakes. Like last night when she was driving us, when we were driving back to the house to finish packing, she missed her turn."

Children may not be saying anything specific about the divorce, but they know the divorce is stressful for their parents. Some children may become very protective of their mother or father, taking on a responsibility to be their emotional caretaker. Parents should discourage this from happening. Parents naturally want their children's support but should not use them as a confidant. That is what friends are for.

Parents come in all sizes, shapes, and personalities. Sometimes, parents are very intellectual and not warm or fuzzy people. This makes talking to your child and getting past their wall of silence particularly difficult. The targeted parent will be more effective if he or she is able to honestly and sincerely share their remorse or hurt about the divorce without becoming overly passionate. Some parents have a great deal of difficulty communicating at this level. Instead, they become very intellectual and analytical or overly zealous which tends to push children away. Children do not know how to react to an overly zealous parent. In response, they may just shut down, or go blank. Younger child can get scared. The child should not feel lectured or talked down to. The cold or aloof parent needs coaching to share their feelings rather than being overly intellectual. The yeller needs to learn better self-control.

Tip: No one likes to talk or listen to a screamer.

The parents may need coaching from the therapist about how to respond to the severely alienated child. The therapist will instruct the targeted parent to avoid blaming the alleged alienating parent, to control passion, avoid becoming defensive and over-analytical, respect the relationship your child has with the other parent, and don't discuss ex-spousal issues. Other lessons to learn are focusing more on listening than talking, not criticizing the other parent's parenting skills, being flexible and considering alternative points of view before responding, and being more positive than negative with the children. Some parents will learn to be more soft and tender rather than cold or intellectual. Obsessed parents may have to be coaxed to cooperate with the counselor. He or she has to believe that the therapist is not aligned with the other parent and that there is something to gain by their participation. Saying that the counseling will help the child is an argument that usually doesn't work because they believe what is best for the child is for the other parent to disappear.

The reunification therapist will help both parents strengthen the relationship with the children. The custodial parent may believe that there is nothing wrong with how they relate to the children, and he or she may be right. Just because a parent is the custodial parent does not mean the relationship cannot be improved. Rather than shutting down, both parents will learn new ways of communicating with the children, reassuring them that they are cared for and loved. Children, without saying so, want to hang on the remnants of the original family. This is not realistic, but can be an issue for some children. After all, they too are grieving for the loss. They too feel they have no control or influence over what is happening. Other children may say that life is better because they no longer hear their parents arguing. Their feelings are understandable.

....

Tip: Both parents can learn how to be better parents.

....

There are ways both parents can strengthen the relationship and help the healing. One child wisely said that, "If you can love me, I can love you back." You are responsible to make this happen, not your children.

- Do not shut down your emotions. You can share your feelings but stop if the child appears distracted or disinterested. You could be saying more than what is necessary.

- Find ways of venting your bitterness to a close friend, family member, or counselor rather than at your children. Venting is alienating and can poison the children's relationship with significant others around them.

- Talk and, more importantly, *listen* to what your children have to say; speak softly, look them in the eye. They need your permission to speak honestly. You may not agree with what the children say, and that has to be okay. Do not be surprised about what you may hear. You can gently clear up any misinformation that they offer, but do not argue with them. Do not force them to agree with your beliefs.

- Do not attack the other parent; doing this will only hurt you.

- Do not do or say anything to cause your child to be alienated from the other parent. Remember the ramifications of the divorce can linger with the children for years.

- When your child gets mouthy or irrational, for the time being ignore what they say. When they are in that mood, you are not going to reason with them. Teens get moody in ways that likely have nothing to do with alienation. Do not blame the other parent for what is a normal developmental issue. Don't push your children to talk or react to you when they shut down. You will make matters worse.

- During a divorce or separation, sometimes children get distracted from school work and their grades go down. Do not blame the ex-spouse for what is happening. Your theory could be wrong. Address the issue as a parenting issue and give your child more help with school work.

- End your discussions with pleasant and meaningful thoughts.

You may ask yourself, "How do I know that I am doing what is right?" The answer is on your child's face or in the tone of his or her voice. After your conversation, you should be able to describe your child's feelings. If not, then you have more parenting to do; you should know what I mean. In addition, if the course of the conversation leaves you feeling more at peace instead of feeling upset, you are heading in the right direction. This is also true for your children. Watch their eyes and tone of voice. That will tell you how you are doing.

Parents are rightfully nervous when considering having their children participate in reunification therapy. This is a reasonable concern. The focus of the therapy is on the parents but the therapist can ask to see the children to assess how therapy is progressing. The therapist's responsibility is to assure both parents that the children's ability to cope with the therapy is closely monitored. It may be helpful for parents to remember that dealing successfully with adversity builds self-esteem. The role of the responsible parent is not to protect the children from all adverse situations but instead to monitor the children's activities so they do not get into a situation that is over their head and beyond their ability to cope.

You should ask the therapist if you have questions about how your child is coping with the therapy.

Assessment

You are not expected to be a therapist after reading this or the next chapter. The chapters will give you some insight about what to expect from therapy and ideas about what you can do now to improve your relationship with the children. You as well as your children will participate in the assessment that will take a few sessions because the parties are interviewed alone and together.

> Tip: Do not expect to sit in with your child and the therapist during the assessment.

The therapist will conduct a thorough assessment to determine the causes of the conflicts and to understand the child's resistance before a reunification plan is developed. The therapist gathers information from extensive interviews with both parents and the children, observes the child's interaction with both parents, completes a thorough psychosocial history, and perhaps administers psychological tests. If previous evaluations have been completed, you can expect to sign a number of releases of information to supplement the assessment. The information can include academic and medical records if there is reason to believe the material is relevant.

Alienation is not the only explanation for the family's dysfunction. Estrangement has to be considered along with determining the extent alienation contributes to the parent-child hostilities. For the purposes of this book, estrangement encompasses all issues that can cause a parent/child conflict other than alienation. Frequently the problems in the family during litigation are a combination of alienation and estrangement. The therapist will investigate all possible reasons for the hostilities and family dysfunction:

- Allegations of physical abuse.
- Allegations of sexual abuse.
- Neglect.
- Ineffective or punitive parenting.
- Failure to bond.

- Serious mental illness.

- Substance abuse.

These concerns are taken into consideration before developing a treatment plan. If any identified issues require an intervention beyond the scope of reunification, the therapist will address the concerns with the parents and make the necessary referral. During the interviews with the parents and children, the therapist will investigate in detail for points of misunderstanding, irrational beliefs, core beliefs held by the parents that relate to the parent's self-esteem or personal identity, cognitive distortions, the presence of alienating behaviors in each parent, and symptoms of parental alienation syndrome in the child. While gathering the information, the therapist will formulate a treatment plan with goals and objectives and proposed treatment interventions. He or she, with the parents, will develop a list of the realities that the parents must accept and cannot change. Both parents have a right to participate in developing the treatment plan and to understand the risks and benefits of the treatment interventions. Developing the treatment plan with the parents is therapeutic because a parent's resistance will quickly become apparent.

Tip: Do not hesitate to ask the therapist questions about any aspect of your treatment, issues of confidentiality, and informed consent.

Throughout the assessment, the therapist begins building a rapport and trust with both parents and the children. The therapist must remain neutral, so you should not expect to have the therapist take your side. The therapist walks a tightrope not to offend anyone. The parents frequently struggle to trust the therapist's fairness and are easily offended, making the therapist's job particularly difficult. The therapist must move slowly. Many therapies fail because one parent believes that the therapist has taken "a side" or because the parent feels maligned by the therapist.

Tip: You must be patient. How much time do you think it will take before you see significant improvement? Your answer is probably not long enough. The longer the time you and your ex-spouse have been hostile with each other before the divorce, the longer you can expect it will take before you see improvement.

The therapist will help both parents understand how his or her behavior is symptomatic of alienation. Do not be offended if you learn that you, too, have engaged in alienating behavior. The naive alienating parent may be very surprised and feel guilty at this news. The obsessed parent may get very defensive and not want to hear what the therapist has to say. The child's statements may corroborate the targeted parent's allegations and the therapist's perceptions. The therapist must work through both parents' defenses by creating an area of psychological safety.

Reunification Therapy

Reunification is about reducing the child's fears and rebuilding the child's relationship with both parents. Admittedly, this is not always possible. First, the alienated parent must have an opportunity to access the child for this to happen. Access may be under very controlled conditions to get the child and the alienating parent's cooperation. A court order may require some mechanism to monitor the alienating parent's compliance to the order, with significant consequence for failure to comply. The order should specifically state that both parents must participate. Reunification is a two-prong process: one process for treating the parents, and the other for monitoring the child's response to the parent's treatment.. Success is measured by how the children respond to both parents. This could include increased parenting time, more loving and spontaneous interaction with the alienated parent, exchanging information between parents, spending time with the extended family, and participating in the child's extracurricular activities. The therapist, while developing the treatment plan, will ask both parents how they will measure success.

Tip: You must be patient during the reunification. Reunification can take months.

The court will stop visits or parenting time if there are allegations of risks to the child's safety while spending unsupervised parenting time with the person they say they hate or fear. Courts are very conservative and are cautious until these types of allegations are resolved. The court does not want to expose children to the threat of physical or sexual abuse or a parent trying to influence the child's possible testimony if the case draws attention to the prosecutor. Someone has to make the judgment about how to protect the child until the allegations are investigated and resolved.

Tip: Do not expect a self-serving parent to fix the problems between the child and the alienating parent.

Courts frequently argue that children of a certain age should decide for themselves when to visit a parent. Parents may argue about when the child is old enough to make that decision. Judges have different opinions about what is a suitable age for making this decision. In the past, many states had the concept of "age of election," meaning that the child at a certain age can decide where they want to live. Age fourteen was a common standard. Legislators wisely recognized that this is not good for children because the law required the child to publicly reject a parent. This clearly put the child in the middle of a tug of war between two opposing parents. Many laws have changed, allowing the children to express a preference but leaving the decision to the court using the best-interest standard. Some children's rights advocates argue against eliminating the age of election, advocating that children should have a right to the decision about where they want to live. The argument implies that the child has sufficient maturity to make the decision.

Tip: Children should not be given the impression that they have a choice when they have no choice. Not having a choice because of a court order is a reality that everyone has to accept. It is the parent's responsibility to see that the child complies with the court order.

It is difficult to know if a child's decision was made without the alienating parent's influences. Courts and evaluators have to consider the child's age and maturity when judging the child's reasons. Hearing the child say, "I have more fun at Dad's [or Mommy's] house" does not carry much weight.

Tip: Do not expect time alone to heal the damage between the alienated child and rejected parent without aggressive intervention when the child lives with an obsessed parent.

The court or the therapist has to determine if reunification is appropriate for the child before the therapy begins. If the child has serious emotional problems, these issues may have to be addressed first in another setting at another time. Questionable allegations of abuse or neglect may require investigation. Therapy could implicitly suggest to a child that his assertions are false when they are true. This can be severely damaging to a child, and for that matter, the parent. If the independent investigation finds nothing to substantiate the allegations, the therapist has to be careful about how they approach abuse when it is mentioned in the session. The therapist may have to return the case to the court if he or she determines that reunification is not currently appropriate. An independent investigation by the local children's service agency is required to address new allegations of abuse. Reunification may have to be put on hold until the results of the investigation are completed

If asked or if the court orders you to participate in reunification therapy, you must comply or your refusal may be held against you. The alienating parent may resent the order and the targeted parent could feel humiliated by the order. You may have to swallow your pride, but is it not your goal to repair the relationship with your child? You also have to be open to the idea that you may be contributing to the problem. Estrangement can be an issue. The therapist will ask you to look at your behavior rather than spending time blaming the other parent and arguing about how you were unjustly treated by the court. All of this may be true, but arguing will not win you any points with the therapist.

> "Well, part of the thing that frustrates me with the divorce stuff is that my mom says I can't go and see one of my friends when I am with her because my friend's mom is friends with my dad."

I mentioned before that the focus of the therapy is on the parents while the child's participation is to monitor progress and for the therapist to understand the child's perspective. This requires the child to participate in the therapy though the therapist will spend significantly more time with the parents, either together or separately.

The reunification therapist has many challenges working with your angry or frightened child. Your child is not in therapy by choice. He or she may resent both of you for forcing him or her into therapy. This situation is especially true for teenagers. The therapist will move slowly, trying to build rapport and trust. Initially, the alliance between the therapist and child is very fragile. Your child will quickly reject any therapist if he or she believes that the therapist is an agent, advocating for the alienated parent. If your child has emotional or serious behavioral problems, the challenge becomes even more formidable. The therapist may determine that the child's problems are caused by normal separation anxiety, oppositional behavior, fears for the alienating parent's welfare, or serious emotional or physical problems of a family member or significant other. A referral for another therapist may be necessary to work on these issues rather than reunification. This is to avoid problems with confidentiality and a possible dual relationship. The longer your child has been angry and refused to see the targeted parent, the longer you can expect the therapy to last.

Tip: Change occurs in small steps. Expect occasional setbacks.

How you and the therapist approach reunification will depend on the child's age and the depth of the anger. Unhampered, younger children are more amenable to change. Older children can be more resistant to change, especially if you, the therapist, and your child get in a power struggle of wills. Building rapport and trust takes considerable time for a child who is dragged to therapy. Work with the therapist; you must contain your enthusiasm and not push for quick results.

Tip: Your child's response to reunification will set the pace for therapy, not you.

When the therapist first meets the child, he or she will make every effort to help the child relax and feel comfortable during the interview. Having already interviewed both parents before meeting the child, the therapist will have an idea about what to expect and will know the issues that will upset the child. Sometimes, a young child will insist that a parent sit in on the first interview while the therapist explains reunification therapy, confidentiality, and offers reassurance that he or she will not be asked to do or say anything that is uncomfortable. Children should be told that they are in control of what they say without the fear of being pressured by anyone. They may have to be assured about their safety.

Beginning in the early sessions, the therapist works to understand the child's fears and the family dynamics and identifies the irrational beliefs and any distortion of reality. A helpful tool for you and the therapist is introducing the child to a SUDS scale (Wolpe 1992) that provides a simple way for the child to feed back the intensity of the anxiety they are feeling in any given situation. The therapist introduces the scale by explaining that anxiety can be rated on a scale from 0 to 100, 100 being the situation when you experienced the most intense anxiety in your life. The therapist will ask for an example: 0 is when the child feels the most relaxed while being awake; 50 is when you first become aware of being nervous, feeling a fluttering in your stomach or sweaty palms. Using this scale, the therapist can ask the child for immediate feedback on the amount of anxiety they feel in a given situation. The therapist works with the child to reduce the child's SUDS level with the targeted parent.

> Tip: Time rarely heals all wounds while the child is living with an alienating parent.

A wise therapist will not be manipulative and try to take on the role of the child's gatekeeper, so do not expect the therapist to make custody or parenting time recommendations. There is an ethical standard (American Psychological Association 1994) that a therapist should not engage in a dual relationship, meaning they cannot function in these two roles: a therapist and an independent evaluator responsible for recommending to the court custody or parenting time. To save time and expense for the parents, it is helpful if the court assigns someone similar to a parent coordinator with arbitration authority to monitor progress and modify parenting time when there is progress. Both parents and the child need to understand that the therapist will not make these recommendations.

Angry children may adhere to very irrational beliefs to the point that the beliefs are delusional. This is not to say they are psychotic or mentally ill. This only means that the child will adhere to irrational beliefs that are contrary to any objective evidence. They are not interested in truth and honesty. As a result, the therapist will likely focus more on strengthening the parent/child relationship rather than reframing or changing irrational beliefs.

The therapist may learn during the initial assessment that the child has estrangement issues with the rejected parent that may have to be treated in a different therapeutic forum, especially if the parent has a personality disorder or a mental illness. The reunification therapist will make that decision. Some children may have experienced or witnessed traumatic events causing severe anxiety or a clinical depression. For a parent, this type of problem can be difficult to detect because the child may appear well-adjusted and coping normally with all that has happened. On the inside, your child could be tied in a knot. You must be receptive to the recommendation by the reunification therapist that your child needs his or her own therapist to work on these issues.

> Tip: Issues other than for the purpose of reunification should be treated by another therapist.

Whether you succeed in rebuilding a relationship depends on your attitude and behavior toward both your child and his parent. Fixing the problems is complex because of the family dynamics, the parents' personalities, the child's resolve and disposition, and the secondary gains from sabotaging the reunification. There are some conditions that both parents must understand and agree to if they want the child/parent reunification to succeed.

- Do not break promises. This can be difficult, because you may casually agree to do something but to your child that is a promise you need to keep. Be careful what you say you are going to do.

- The alienated child is a victim, like you. Do not blame your child.

- Expect to work with the child's other parent during the reunification therapy.

- Significant others may have to participate in the therapy. The therapists will make that decision.

- Do not expect your child to agree with your point of view or arguments about why you feel slighted. Your child does not want to hear your arguments. Pressuring your child to agree with your arguments is putting him or her in the middle, having to choose sides. In the end, you will likely lose.

- Try empathizing with your child. Try putting yourself in your child's shoes and understanding what that feels like.

- You need to learn to listen to your child without getting defensive. Do not deny their hurt or anger. Thinking about what you are going to say next is not listening to your child. You may have to apologize for your behavior.

- When your child makes an accusation against you because of what he or she is told, you can emphasize to your child that he has a right to draw his own opinions, based on his experiences rather than what he is told. You can say, "Honey, I know what you hear can be confusing, but I have confidence that whatever you believe should be from your own experience rather than what you are told." Children, particularly ones who are older, need to know that you encourage them to think for themselves. Therapists call this *individuation*, a process when the child learns to accept opinions separate from their parents. This is all part of the child developing their own identity, a sense of who they are separate from the parents. This can be very trying for the parents, but it's a healthy process for the child. What is not healthy is a child that feels so enmeshed with a parent that the child cannot individuate. This is very noticeable with the severely alienated child because their belief may be in lockstep with the alienating parent. What the alienating parent says is what the child must believe. This is a common trait of the severely alienated child who is enmeshed with an obsessed parent.

Rebuilding a relationship is more than talking about what not to do. Sometimes, common sense tells us what not to do, like yelling, swearing, and screaming at our children. Mentoring is a frame of mind that will help redefine the type of relationship you have with your children.

Treating the Anxiety and Fear

Your child must have his or her anxiety under control if reunification is to be successful. Dr. Joseph Wolpe (1992) in the 1970s developed a thera-peutic technique called *systematic desensitization,* which is used to reduce a patient's phobias, and irrational fears. Weitzman (2004) adapted Wolpe's desensitization and applied the technique to reduce an alienated child's anxiety or fear toward a targeted parent. Though he has no outcome data, his approach is theoretically sound. The treatment approach is to gradually introduce the child to the targeted parent in small steps where the child is not overwhelmed by the anxiety level. Using Weitzman's approach, the child is initially exposed to the targeted parent's picture, the voice, and then observes the parent behind a one-way window listening to the parent answer questions prepared by the child. The child learns to relax, receiving assurance from the therapist, correcting cognitive distortions, and taking successive steps to keep the anxiety level manageable. The therapist may introduce techniques that help the child to inhibit the anxiety like active play, relaxation techniques, or a mental rehearsal with a more positive outcome.

Courts try to use a similar approach when they order supervised visits. The problem is the lack of progressive steps in the court order that allows for a gradual exposure of the child to the targeted parent. Counseling may be ordered, but the order typically does not include a mechanism for adjusting the child's exposure to the parent and increasing the parenting time. Someone has to have this authority other than the therapist. Therapy is an evolving process that requires flexibility and being sensitive to how the child is progressing. Court orders do not consider changes in the chil-dren, their maturation, or the family dynamics.

During the desensitization, the parent may require instruction on parenting and how to strengthen the bond. Parenting is complex, especially if you have limited time with your children. The therapist will identify your parenting shortcomings and give you instruction to enhance your effectiveness.

If you are not involved in therapy with your alienated child, there are ways you can help to reduce your child's fears. Begin by ensuring that you have access to your child in a psychologically safe environment. This may require a court order if the obsessed parent insists on interfering with your parenting time. The environment may not be your home but instead a fun location like Chuck E. Cheese, a ballgame, ice skating, bowling, or an activity that you know has been fun for your child in the past and can be distracting. The activity should be age appropriate and something that your child enjoys, not an activity that only suits your interest. Just because you enjoy camping does not mean that your son will share your interest. Further, do not have your significant other present during this time. This is time for only you and the children. You must have patience and must not expect to spend all the time together you would like. Always end the time together on a positive note, before your child gets tired or bored.

Disciplining

Many weekend parents are afraid to discipline, fearing that the children will run to the other parent and complain or worse yet, not return. In turn, the custodial parent criticizes the weekend parent for letting the children run wild and feels resentful that they have to be the bad guy for the responsibility to discipline. Parenting has added challenges after a separation or divorce. Neither parent wants the children to see them as the bad guy. When parents refuse to communicate about parenting and values, the children suffer. This is not to say the parents have to agree; they do not. A divorce has its own problems when it comes to disciplining the children. Discipline begins by having the child understand the rules you dictate. The rules do not have to be the same as the other parent's. Children in time learn to discriminate between the households as to what is expected of them. In fairness, they should know the rules before they are violated.

Problem behavior must be put into perspective. Parents can damage relationships with their children if they make a big deal about everything. Some parents react to the smallest problems with great intensity. You will be better off if you learn to prioritize your child's behaviors that need to be addressed and know what behaviors for the time being to ignore. You can learn to tone down your reactions by following this simple exercise to put problems in perspective. The exercise goal is for you to judge your child's behaviors on a scale from zero to ten; ten being extremely serious behavior that threatens one's safety or lifestyle, and zero having no more importance beyond deciding what to eat. Going through this process gives the parent time to regain control over their feelings and also allows them to think and put the problem into perspective. Parents may be surprised how many issues are insignificant after completing this simple exercise. This exercise works for other situations that you find yourself emotionally reacting to. Try the exercise—you may be surprised how well this works.

You have to consider your child's age, maturity, and their ability to communicate and reason when considering your rules and discipline. Parents sometimes have the erroneous belief that a verbal child is also a reasoning child and should be able to think before acting. They should be able to anticipate the consequences of their behavior. This is not true for young children. Young children do not have the ability to empathize and anticipate consequences of their behavior other than "Am I going to be punished?" To help you understand, consider this example. When you go for a job interview, you rehearse in your mind what you are going to say and how to behave. Preteens do not have this ability to anticipate or rehearse in their mind how to behave. Children of all ages continually struggle with learning to contain their impulsive behavior and think before acting. You can see that understanding your child's development is very complex. You must be patient and realistic about what you expect from your child. Rules and discipline should be age appropriate.

When parents first learn about their pregnancy, Mom and Dad buy baby books to learn about developmental stages. Most parents learn the age when they can expect their child to take their first step and say their first word. For whatever reason, when the child learns to be verbal, many parents appear to lose interest in understanding child or teenage development. There is a big difference between the number of baby books and books on teenage development in the bookstores. Perhaps the difference is from a lack of interest. You may want to purchase a book to learn more about your older child's development.

Tip: Shift the pathogenic ratio by making it a point to be more positive than critical with your children.

Pathogenic ratio is the proportion of positive or complimentary statements versus critical statements. Like anyone else, children like to be with people who make them feel good about themselves. If you want to keep your relationship strong with your children, the proportion of complimentary statements must exceed critical comments. A desirable ratio to keep the relationship strong is 70 percent positive and 30 percent critical. By the way, the pathogenic ratio applies for any relationship, not just your children. If you want to know how you are doing keeping a relationship strong, ask yourself, "What percentage of my interaction with that person is positive as opposed to negative?" If your percentage is less then 70, you have work to do. You may have to think hard about finding positive attributes, especially with your children.

Sometimes, a parent who has limited time with the children, and who questions the other parent's discipline, will try to make up for poor parenting by being extra critical of the children. This never works and only harms the relationship. Again, consider the pathogenic ratio. You need to praise your children more often than criticize. This positive ratio gives you power to influence your child's behavior because of their desire to please you.

There are other considerations to disciplining.

- If you must criticize, comment on behavior, not character. For example, "Melissa, you know better than to eat ice cream with your fingers" not "Oh, Melissa, you are such a disgusting slob!" Do not call your children derogatory names.

- Do not make negative comparisons between your child and their other parent; this is alienating.

- Always make up after a punishment. Praise your child when they have complied with your punishment. When you must punish or discipline, complete the punishment at least two hours before they go to the other parent's home. Never end a visit during a punishment because the punishment, rather than the good times, is what the child will remember until the next visit. The child may even refuse to go if he or she believes you are angry with them.

- During visits, do not expect to compress all your teachings and discipline into a weekend. This is not only impossible, but it is good reason for children to dread the next visit.

- For better or worse, children are always changing. Keep in mind that behavioral problems are not always caused by the divorce or what occurs in the other household. Whatever the source of the problems, you have to learn how to respond to your child. Yelling and blaming do not work. If the behavior persists, you may talk to the other parent and learn if he or she is seeing the same behavior. Together, you may be able to come up with a parenting strategy to correct the behavior. Rather than blame, speak with concern and a desire to understand the behavior. Decide how you can work together to change the behavior. Children who see their parents working together for their best interest are less likely to manipulate the parents and will adjust better to the divorce. A counselor may help if you and your ex-spouse cannot work together. These issues should come up during reunification therapy.

- Regularly ask yourself, "How effective is the discipline?" Is it only producing short-term results, or is it actually teaching my children to be more responsible and socially conscious individuals? Your child's response to discipline tells you if the discipline works. Remember your goal is to change behavior and not always making your child happy.

Mentoring

You need to know when to mentor and when to punish. Parents typically have an idealized image in their mind of the perfect child. Then there is reality, which often falls short of your ideals. As a parent, you must learn to accept your children for who they are and offer them loving guidance. The children must believe they are valued for their talents and skills rather than feel inadequate for not living up to your ideals. If you cannot think of any of your child's positive attributes, you need to look harder. Remember what you learned about the pathogenic ratio. Imagine how your child must feel if you cannot even think of anything positive to say about them. What kind of energy do you convey in your child's presence? If the tables were turned, would you feel loved? In time, would you care about whether or not you pleased your parents? Do you only want them to comply with your demands because he or she fears you? Your children will want to avoid you if they see you as a source of pain and criticism. This is not due to alienation. You lose your power to bring positive changes in their behavior or influence their values. If you hear from the other parent that your children do not want to visit, think about where your relationship is with the pathogenic scale. You may gain some understanding about what to do if your ratio is negative.

Children are faced every day with new and unique situations that they do not know how to handle because they lack maturity and experience to respond appropriately. Because of their inexperience, children will make poor decisions that could appear to you as if they deliberately misbehaved. This can be confusing for both you and your children. Sometimes you are better off thinking twice about punishment and should instead think about whether your child needs mentoring.

Knowing when to discipline or mentor can be confusing. Disciplining is following through with consequences that your child should have understood before deciding to misbehave. Mentoring is calmly teaching your child how to make better decisions in the future and giving them the tools to make better decisions. You must have your emotions under control while mentoring. Mentoring gives you an opportunity to strengthen the bond with your child while teaching him or her family values and new life skills. Mary's mother is an example of taking advantage of a bad situation to mentor her daughter.

Mary's Story

Mary was noticeably frightened and she knew she had to tell her mother what happened in school today. While waiting for her girlfriend to come out of the classroom, she noticed that Sue was taking something off their teacher's desk. Later in the day, Sue asked Mary to take the designer pen because she believed she was going to get caught. Mary, not knowing what to do, took the pen. Sure enough, both were caught and sent to the principal's office. Wisely, Mary thought she should tell her mother rather than wait for the principal to call. Mary's mother saw how frightened her daughter was. Rather than punish, she decided to mentor her daughter because of the unique quandary she faced. Mary didn't know whether to betray her loyalty to Sue and tell the teacher, or to say nothing, knowing that she had done wrong. Mary's mother understood her daughter's dilemma and reasoned that she needed help on how to make the best decision rather than getting yelled at and grounded. Mary already felt guilty and needed her mother's guidance. How would you have advised your child in this situation?

Tips on Mentoring

- Keep your emotions under control. Use a teacher or counselor as a role model when talking with your child.

- Keep calm and focus on what your child says rather than what you are going to say next.

- Avoid making judgmental statements like, "That's stupid" or "Stop acting like a baby." You will learn about the feedback model in the next chapter.

- Seek clarification about what you do not understand. Ask questions.

- Discuss alternative solutions and consequences.

- Guide your child to a solution.

- Do not humiliate your child in the presence of others, particularly siblings.

- Praise your child for talking out the problem and let him or her know how proud you feel.

Mentoring is a frame of mind, an attitude, and a desire to guide your child. It is not a confrontation, an excuse to blame, or a litany of accusations.

Before following up on a concern voiced by your children, ask yourself whether the matter is really worth discussing with your ex-spouse. Consider first doing the exercise described above about putting behaviors in perspective. Is the issue sufficiently important to risk starting an argument or could you simply reassure your youngsters and move on?

When children tell you something that is inconsistent with what your ex-spouse has said, do not automatically conclude that your kids are correct and your ex-spouse is lying. You may be biased in your desire to believe your children before your ex-spouse, especially if honesty wasn't a strong suit. There could be other explanations for the discrepancy, such as a simple misunderstanding about what the child is saying. In addition, calling your ex-spouse a liar is alienating and will likely provoke a fight when confronted. This is not helpful to the children. Be very careful before believing what your child says and how you react.

This chapter helps to lay the groundwork for reunification. The next chapter will offer you many examples of what you can do to change your behavior, changes that will facilitate reunification. You may find it helpful to think about what you have learned in this chapter before reading the next chapter. There is a lot of information to absorb.

Reunification

"How can I expect to see my children when their father sabotages me at every turn?"

Reunification is complex and may not be easily understood without a mental health background. This chapter is for parents but offers pointers for therapists to consider. Various treatment modalities are summarized to quench the parent's thirst for knowledge about how to change and respond to alienating behavior. However, understanding a theory for change is not the same as changing behavior. Understanding is a start. The material in this chapter is intended to help you understand approaches to reunification therapy. There are many examples of new behaviors that may help reduce hostilities, and protect your children from alienation and, worse yet, from parental alienation syndrome. The material is hypothetical because effective treatment protocols and outcome studies for reunification therapy in general are severely lacking. Very qualified and successful therapists will use treatment methods different from what is described below. You may find that many of the treatment approaches described are helpful for your circumstances. Peer review journal articles (Campbell 1992; Johnston, Walters, and Friedlander 2001; Sullivan and Kelly 2001) describe therapeutic interventions that are theoretically sound, but not validated with outcome studies.

Reading this chapter does not make you a therapist or solve all your problems with alienation. The chapter will not cure the ills of the obsessed parent. Instead, the chapter will enhance your toolbox to improve your communication, reduce the tensions and conflicts with the other parent, and with practice strengthen the relationship with your children.

Therapists vary in their approaches to therapy; there is no one approach that will work in all circumstance. Therapists adapt their interventions depending on how they perceive the issues and information after a thorough assessment. The assessment has to involve speaking to both parents and the children. Therapy is most effective if parents understand the therapeutic process and acknowledge their responsibilities to promote change. Clients learn what they do outside of the therapy is more important than what they do during the sessions.

Tip: If all you want from therapy is affirmation that you are right about the issues rather than sharing responsibility to change, the therapy will fail.

You are more likely to see a change in your child's attitude about spending time with you when he or she sees that you and your ex-spouse are amicably working together. This is the ideal. The reality may be that your child learns to tolerate time with you, but at least that is a start for you to work on rebuilding the relationship. The child's feelings must be considered. The alienating parent must participate in the therapy with the child available to the therapist. You may feel cynical about seeking therapy. But what choice do you have other than trying?

Stepparents or extended family members are very important in the reunification process because they could either support or sabotage the process. Stepparents should not feel left out of the process, though they may not be as actively involved in treatment. The therapist will occasionally need to spend time with the stepparent to assess their feelings, offer reassurance, and to divert any possibilities of sabotage. The therapist may have to work with the stepparent to change his or her attitude about reunification for therapy to succeed.

Tip: The parent and not the stepparent should be in the forefront of the treatment.

The therapist will work to break through the child's wall of silence. Silence is a child's way of avoiding talking about what is uncomfortable, or losing emotional control. Both parents must be prepared for the possibility that once the therapist works through the child's defenses, the child may experience an intense emotional catharsis with displays of rage, tears, or even physical aggression. Both parents, but especially the targeted parent, must be receptive and sensitive to the child's changing emotions. Though reunification can be frightening and guilt-ridden for the parents, they should think of this time as a breakthrough in the child's resistance. Your children's feelings must not be stifled by your defensiveness or desire to rescue them. Your children may need your guidance about how to appropriately express their feelings.

Reunification therapy is stressful for all, including the therapists. Most therapists will limit their caseload to two or three high-conflict families. Parents can be very demanding and quick to blame the therapist if therapy does not favor their own hidden agenda.

Tip: Do not expect to have private phone conversations with the therapist.

A Word of Caution

Parents with mental illness, a history of substance abuse, or personality disorders may experience more severe symptoms during therapy. Depressed patients will become more depressed; anxious parents will become more anxious. Narcissistic parents can become more demanding and angry. Parents with a borderline personality disorder, marked by unstable relationships and intense periods of anger, may rage when their manipulations fail to coax the therapist to their side. The therapist must manage all these issues. The therapist will encourage the parent to continue seeing their primary therapist to treat these issues.

Reunification Therapy

A premise for reunification therapy is very simple to understand but difficult to implement: changing your behavior or thought processes can change how you feel and in turn how you respond to others. Your thought process or cognitive style will influence how you will perceive and interpret events. Your cognitive style will influence your self-talk. A parent's cognitive style can lead to erroneous conclusions, inappropriate responses to events, and poor choices and behaviors. Our beliefs, conclusions, responses, choices, and behaviors lead to feelings, which again feed our self-talk and our behavior.

A struggle for reunification therapists is negotiating the conflicts and interests between the emotional needs of the children and the parents. Children's emotional needs are important to consider but it is the parent's responsibility to be the leader, the children's authority, and to set limits and rules. Targeted parents argue that they not only have the right but also it is in the child's best interest that the therapy focuses on the parent's desire for reunification even when the child resists or refuses to participate. In many jurisdictions, the parent's rights exceed those of the children. Other therapists or activists argue that the children should have a voice, even to the extent of deciding whether they want to participate in reunification therapy. This is subjugating the parent's authority. The child needs to be heard but the assumption that children know better than adults is ridiculous. Another concern is, will children forced to participate in reunification therapy be damaged or is reunification worth the risk when weighed against the possibility of the child never seeing the alienated parent again? How would you answer the question?

There are two flaws with the child directing the therapy. First, children have a propensity to avoid anything that is uncomfortable. In effect, children believe what is "best" for them is what immediately feels most comfortable. Their desire to avoid discomfort and seek immediate gratification bolsters a second concern, whether the child is responsible or mature enough to make decisions regarding their long-term best interest. Children have a very limited capacity to anticipate or understand long-term consequences for their decisions. Therefore, parents frequently have to make decisions for their children, contrary to their wishes. I believe this is equally true regarding their participation with reunification therapy.

The parents' inherent responsibility is to protect their children from impending or future harm. Every day, we make judgments about the risk of our children being harmed if they participate in a particular activity. For example, we do not allow a two-year-old to decide whether to cross the street without supervision. Adults and laws require teenagers to have education and training before they receive their driver's licenses. A parent needs to understand that, not only a child's, but also an adult's self-esteem comes from adequately coping with adversarial events and facing uncomfortable situations. You can't help but take risks allowing your child to take on new challenges. Learning to tolerate failure is not all bad as long as your child is safe.

Rational Belief: Parents, not the children, are the authority.

Robert's Story

The court referred Robert for reunification therapy. He had not seen his two daughters, ages fourteen and sixteen, for over eighteen months. He accused his ex-wife of alienating the children from his affections.

During the interview with the oldest child, she was quite emphatic about her desire to have no relationship with her father. She described in detail how her father had physically victimized her mother. He denied the allegation. The youngest daughter was less vocal. She put up a wall of silence and offered very little about her feelings other than emphatically stating, "I don't want to see my father."

The younger child did not witness the alleged physical assault though she heard about it from her mother and sister. Because of the older daughter's age, the therapist decided to focus the reunification therapy on the younger daughter. The mother showed improvement in that her animosity and anger toward her ex-husband decreased. After a few sessions, she was able to recognize that it was in her younger daughter's best interest to reunify with her father. She was a very agreeable participant in the process. In fact as therapy progressed, she was able to give the father very specific suggestions about how he might build the relationship with his daughter.

The father came a long way in that he accepted the suggestions without getting defensive. He asked very insightful questions. During the fourth session the mother, father, and daughter spent some time outside without the therapist because everyone felt that perhaps the therapist's office heightened the child's anxiety. The father wanted to apologize to his daughter for anything she had seen or heard of his prior aggression. He was very emotional and began to cry. When the daughter saw her father's emotions, she became very tearful though she did not totally drop the wall of silence. Clearly, the father's message got through to her. Though the daughter was quite pained, the therapist and her parents thought this had been somewhat of an emotional breakthrough. The daughter was beginning to perceive her father as a feeling human being.

Interventions

Relationships do not improve overnight. Change may take months if not years. The process can be slow and unfortunately expensive. You may remember that alienation evolved over a long time, perhaps even before the separation. Repairing the damage may take even longer, especially with the severely alienated child or an obsessed parent. The more both parents appreciate the importance of resolving their differences for the children's sake and are motivated to change, the less time and expense will be involved. After all the litigation and expense for both parents, the reality is that neither parent is going to disappear. That reality must be accepted. So, now, you must move forward.

Change is a multifaceted process that can involve an array of therapeutic interventions. The therapist never knows exactly what will work because success is dependent on your motivation and willingness to change your behavior and thinking. The therapist may influence you but cannot change you. If one intervention is ineffective, the therapist will take a different approach. This is also true about what you will learn from this book. A good metaphor emphasizing this point is a physician prescribing a new medication. The physician knows the purpose of the medication but cannot know the medication's effectiveness or side effects until after you take the medication. You have to tell the therapist what is and what is not working. The therapist will strive to establish rapport with the parents and the children, defining the therapist's role as a reunification therapist, and initiating the assessment process to identify cognitive distortions, core distortions, and the distortion style. Confidentiality, privacy, and safety will be discussed.

Laying the Groundwork

Change is a multifaceted process. The goal is to change behavior and attitudes. The foundation for change includes a process to identify unyielding realities that both parents must accept, irrational beliefs that are the foundation for irrational behavior, cognitive distortions or simple misinformation leading to erroneous conclusions, and damaging cognitive styles or how you process information.

Tip: Learning new behavior is not a quick fix for alienation. What you learn about reunification will carry over to all relationships.

Realities

Identifying realities that are true and not negotiable for both parents is the underpinning for the therapy. A reality is a statement of fact that you cannot immediately change. A fact is a law, a birthright, a court order, or a conclusion supported by the preponderance of research. Realities are important because parents have to reconcile in their minds how to live with the realities governing their situation and not hurt the children. Every decision and choice always goes back to not hurting the children. Changes made by parents must include reconciling realities that they and the children have to live with. The realities that are true for most parents are:

- Most state laws are very specific in stating that both parents have a right to be involved in raising and caring for their children.

- Whether a parent likes it or not, the court orders and parenting plans are facts that both parents must accept unless they return to court to change the orders.

- Continued hostilities, parental in-fighting, and protracted litigation hurt children. The therapist should be able to provide the parents with studies supporting this reality.

- Children adjust better to a divorce when they have a reciprocal and loving relationship with both parents.

- Neither parent is going to disappear from the child's life.

- Parents not only share in their children's lives, but they will share in the grandchildren's lives. Parenting does not end simply because adults decide to end their relationship. Both parents will be in each other's face for the rest of their lives. It helps if the parents avoid frowns, angry expressions, or blatant hatred as they continue to parent their children. Active parents may share in their children's schooling, graduations, holidays, get-togethers, weddings, religious ceremonies, and even family funerals. Children should not learn over the years to dread these occasions because of the parents' hostilities and fear of being embarrassed by their parents' behavior.

If you stop and think about your situation, don't these realities apply to you and your children? Accepting these realities is not the same as liking the realities. You can accept facts without necessarily liking them. Change requires both parents to accept the realities that apply to them and the children. You need to identify additional realities that apply to your situation, such as: financial limitations, family health problems, aging parents or grandparents, childcare, or your child's mental health.

Exercise: Realities

List any additional realities that you believe apply to you and the other parent that must be reconciled for both of you to parent successfully.

_____

_____

_____

During the course of therapy, your therapist will frequently remind you of the realities to keep you on track with what you are trying to accomplish. An example is one parent saying that the other parent should walk away from their child because their child doesn't want to see him ever again. The therapist will remind the alienating parent that this is not going to happen because father is not going away. Given this reality, the issue is how the alienating parent and child are going to accept and work with this reality. During the early course of therapy, there will be frequent reminders, each time frustrating the alienating parent and child, when he or she is also reminded of the realities.

Challenging or arguing with your ex-spouse to change his or her beliefs will not work, even if they hold erroneous or irrational beliefs. If the two of you are arguing about alienation or access to your children, it is likely that your ex-spouse will not trust what you have to say and will refuse to suffer the humiliation of admitting you are right, even if you *are* right. A reunification therapist, brought into the fray by court order, can help both parties come to terms with unchangeable realities and can be particularly helpful to an obsessed parent. You can begin by not getting manipulated into arguing. A reunification therapist can also help parents evaluate their personal realities, strike agreements, and initiate change. For example, both parents may need to face a decreased income or availability of spending money. There is no sense arguing about realities you cannot change. The parents may need to compromise about how much to spend on braces or dance sessions, or agreements to create a savings plan for the children's college.

Understanding and accepting common realities is needed before constructive change can occur. Both parents must find a common ground believing that they do not want to harm the children. This has to be the parent's motivation for change, to not hurt the children any more than what has already occurred. Perhaps, this is the first reality they share in common. Any time parents refuse to accept or argue about one of the fixed realities, the argument should revert to how harmful this is to the children. For some parents, this point may have to be driven home repeatedly. Parents with a severe personality disorder find this particularly difficult because they cannot separate their own irrational beliefs from the children's best interests. They strive to continue their enmeshment with the child for fear of losing control.

The therapist will educate both parents about how continued high-conflict, protracted litigation, and hostilities hurt children for many years to come, if not forever. Like it or not, both parents must face this reality as a starting point for healthy relationships with their children. Together, you will identify the harsh realities that both of you must accept. Reunification therapy is about the children. It is not about the parents' selfish needs to have what they want or to use the children as a vehicle for revenge.

Many of the unyielding realities have to be accepted by both parents. Every time the reality is raised, the parent needs reminding that you cannot change the reality but must accept the reality, otherwise children are hurt. This is repeated time and time again.

After identifying the realities and at least for the time being understanding that these realities are not going to change, the process for change can begin. There are many different protocols for bringing about change in how parents and children will learn to think and behave, while learning to reconcile the realities that all must live with so as to not hurt the children. You are about to read many methods therapists use to bring about change. Though I may be addressing the therapist, the methods are written in a way for parents to understand and use the material. Some of the methods will be easier to understand and can be easily practiced without involving a therapist. Be patient and give yourself time to practice what you learn.

Fundamentals for Change

Flawed thinking can extremely damage you and your children. However, most people are unaware, for the most part, of when their own flawed thinking interferes with relationships. Sometimes, friends and family bring to our attention the problems in our thinking. We may feel attacked, we may rebel, or we might stop and think about just what we do think.

Most people need help from a professional to fully understand why certain thinking is, indeed, "flawed." Trying to recognize your flawed thinking requires an openness to look deeply inside yourselves. Changing how we process information and learning to recognize our own flawed thinking is very difficult. You must be receptive to the therapist's feedback because he or she will recognize the flawed thinking better than what we see in ourselves. Recognizing our cognitive distortions and learning to change our thought processes will result in far more rational behavior. Remember, our feelings are the result of how we behave and what we believe to be true. If your thought processes, or how you process information, is faulty, you will come to erroneous conclusions and likely feel worse than times when you used more rational thinking.

People usually define themselves in three ways. First, our core beliefs influence our self-esteem and define who we think we are. For example, the core belief of believing we are either a good or bad parent dramatically influences how we think about ourselves and how we act. "As my daughter's mother, I always know what is best" or "Being a man, I am the best person to raise my sons" are ideas that affect how each parent behaves and the decisions each makes. "I'm no good at anything, even parenting" or "My kids will just follow my bad example" can undermine a parent's drive to be a better parent or to parent at all. Additionally, a parent with low self-esteem often has trouble changing self-perceptions when she is constantly belittled. This parent may need more support through personal therapy. She may need to learn a whole new way of looking at and defining herself if she has been a victim of domestic violence.

Second, specific cognitive styles describe how an individual processes information. Making assumptions, catastrophic thinking, and dichotomous thinking are a few examples of cognitive styles that can lead to erroneous conclusions. When a dad uses catastrophic thinking, he may feel paralyzed by his constant fears and find it hard to change this thinking style. When a mom creates chaos through dichotomous thinking, she may be unaware of how her cognitive style affects interactions with others.

Third, cognitive distortions and erroneous beliefs influence behavior. If a parent believes certain falsehoods about parenting (or about other people's motivations or intentions), these beliefs can cause irrational behavior. For example, if a father believes that his homosexual spouse may cause their daughter to become homosexual, or if a mother believes that men cannot change a diaper, these beliefs may cause the parent to refuse visitation or to make untrue accusations against the other parent. Very often, people defend their erroneous beliefs, not realizing how irrational the beliefs may seem to others.

Core Beliefs

Core beliefs are about who we are and define our self-esteem. How do you describe yourself? Are you a loving and compassionate person, ethical, moral, a hard worker, sensitive to others, or a good parent? We all have a self-perception and a preference for how we want others to see us. Our idealized self is not the same as our real self as seen by others. When we feel our core beliefs as being attacked—those beliefs that shore up our self-esteem—we naturally become defensive and are fueled for the counter-attack. This is the reason why court is so painful, because we will hear our core beliefs attacked and yet we are expected to remain quiet and just take it. This is true for everyone, not just parents going through a divorce.

Core beliefs are "I" statements: "I am a good and loving parent, I am a caring person, I am a hard worker." Being told that you are lazy, an abusive parent, or an unloving parent are attacks on your core beliefs and will incite anger and defensiveness.

Both parents approach therapy with their personal collection of core beliefs. Each tries to give the therapist a good impression, hoping to receive positive affirmation that reinforces their core belief about what a wonderful parent they are. Core beliefs are powerful motivators. Core beliefs are issues for both the alienating and targeted parent and can be obstacles for change. Common for some target parents is the struggle to quit pursuing a relationship with their children because others (the child, the families) believe him as an unloving and uncaring parent. Mothers choosing to give up custody often feel stigmatized because they imagine others will question "How can a mother who loves her children give up custody?" The question attacks the mother's core belief. The vast majority of parents want to believe that they are loving and good parents, even when they are not. The reunification therapist may not be the best therapist to help the parent with irrational core beliefs if they are interlinked with a personality disorder. A referral may be necessary. The reunification therapist has to be very cautious about the timing and the means of suggesting the referral, for fear that the parent will bolt from therapy.

Parents suffering from a mental disorder or personality disorder can be especially difficult when confronted with their irrational core beliefs. A parent believing they would be an incompetent parent for not protecting their children from imagined risk of sexual or physical abuse could perceive an attack on their core belief and this may cause the parent to prematurely terminate therapy. The therapist must be very cautious working with core beliefs and must move very slowly. The targeted parent, while these issues are being dealt with, has to be patient.

Cognitive Distortions

Cognitive distortions or misinformation originates from your personal experiences, past learnings, and personal biases about how you judge information that you have learned. This is important to understand because your reactions to the divorce, your ex-spouse, and children are influenced by information you have learned in the past. What you have come to believe as a truth (such as: a good mother knows better than a father how to raise children) will influence how the mother feels when the children are in the father's care. The anxiety may be unwarranted. Another example of how misinformation influences our feelings and decisions is that adolescent males should not cry or girls do poorly with science and mathematics. Other cognitive distortions or misinformation that can influence how sons and daughters are raised include:

- Children are always better off with their mothers.
- Children always know best about where they want to live.
- Fathers know nothing about how to parent.
- Once an abuser, always an abuser.

You may agree that these statements are true and expect others, like school counselors or evaluators, to share your opinions. Your flawed thinking leads to irrational behavior such as denigrating your son for crying, arguing that fathers cannot learn to change a diaper, or discouraging your daughter from becoming a scientist.

Irrational belief: I must prove that I am always the more competent parent. I can never admit to doing anything wrong, especially to my ex-spouse.

Behavior that is hurtful to self and others is irrational. From a distorted reality follows mistaken conclusions and a parent making poor choices. Realities are objective facts, even if we wish those facts were different. Male children and adults *do* cry without demeaning their masculinity and woman *are* successful researchers. There are presently more females than males in medical schools. Masculine sport figures are seen crying on television. These are realities that cannot be denied. Women are capable of learning science. With the therapist's help and education, you will learn to identify and overcome the obstacles or cognitive distortions that interfere with your rational thinking and perhaps explain your inappropriate behavior.

Irrational Thinking: "I could never live with myself if I agree to give Jimmy's father custody. I know I have a drug problem but a father cannot love a child like a mother."

Every day we hear in the news the results from some study dispelling a myth. For example, we know that teenage boys can be victims of sexual abuse (Wallace 2002). This is one example of a myth that was corrected by a study. It is no longer correct to assume that only females and not males can be victims of sexual abuse. Studies and even the news media provide new information that has forced us to daily change our thinking. Who is not surprised to see in recent years the number of female teachers who have had sexual relationships with adolescent males? As a result of the incidents, society has become more accepting that both boys and girls are victims of sexual abuse.

To help recognize cognitive distortions or misinformation, the therapists must be current on the research about families and children embroiled in high-conflict relationships. Therapists may find it helpful to compile a notebook of studies documenting how high conflict hurts children and families. Understanding the local judicial system is a must for the therapist because many parents are ill equipped to tackle the court's intricacies. This is a reality. Without acting like an attorney, parents sometimes need clarification about the judicial process in their community. Good research and the law must be the foundation supporting the therapist and parent's reality. Whether we agree with the law or the results of the studies is not the issue. The therapist and parent must accept the same reality. Remember, reality is what the parent or the therapist cannot change. Allowing the parent to review the material can be a powerful motivator (impending catastrophe) for change. You need to have an open mind and realize the possibility that what you learn is in your child's best interest.

State laws and court orders are another important source of information defining reality. In most states, both mother and father are on equal footing when it comes to initially assigning custody. The reality is that custody is given to the mother 85 to 90 percent of the time. Whether the parent disagrees or believes that the court order is unfair doesn't matter. Until the order or state law is changed, the order is reality. End of discussion.

Education

Education is very effective for correcting misinformation, removing obstacles to change, and helping the parent to accept the realities. Naive and active alienating parents are more amenable to education than are obsessed parents. Like the examples above, the therapist will help parents identify misinformation that adversely influences their behavior and feelings.

However, education alone rarely works for the obsessed alienator because of their rigid beliefs. They cannot accept what the therapist says without getting defensive. They want to challenge the veracity of the reality. What they want from the therapist is affirmation that their position is correct and their self-esteem is not attacked. Any challenge places the therapist on the enemy list. The therapist must often be repetitive with the obsessed alienator while being careful not to offend. Sometimes information and education couched in metaphors and legitimate compliments will lessen the obsessed alienator's defensiveness.

I am frequently surprised how often conflicts between parents get resolved after they have expressed their thoughts and feelings and then receive a little education from their attorney. Parents need to tell their story and be heard. In court, parents are frequently frustrated when ushered into a small waiting room, instructed by their attorney to remain quiet and wait for the attorneys to come out of the courtroom, and then are told how others want to manage their lives and their children's lives. Parents want and need to tell their story. They need a trusted attorney to identify and then replace cognitive distortions with accurate information. Attorneys need time educating their clients about the litigation. Parents want to know the strengths and weaknesses of their case. Parents may not like what they hear, but it is the attorneys' responsibility to convey reality.

Tip: Education from a trusted individual is very powerful.

Parents may ask, "What is the difference between a cognitive distortion and reality?" Therapists may find this a difficult question to answer. Therapists, like anyone else, have cognitive distortions or misinformation. They may offer information like it is absolute truth when in truth they are wrong. This is especially true if the therapist advocates a political agenda.

Therapists are trained to recognize their biases and irrational beliefs. Training in cultural diversity is intended to destroy myths and irrational thinking that can adversely influence how the therapist relates to people from different cultural backgrounds. You may wonder how this applies to you. During the course of evaluations, I am seeing more parents laboring over the knowledge that their son or daughter and maybe even the ex-spouse have a sexual orientation very different from their own. Culturally or racially mixed relationships are becoming more common. A parent adjusting to these changes in cultural norms may experience considerable anxiety if he or she has not been personally exposed to these aspects of our changing culture.

Resistance toward shared parenting and negativity toward a father's more active participation in raising their children continues because of the sustained belief of the "tender years" doctrine. Many judges, contrary to state laws, do not believe in their hearts that a father is as capable as a mother, or even a grandmother, in competently raising and caring for a child, particularly if the child is under the age of two. Slowly the "tender years" doctrine is giving way to the "best interest of the child" doctrine through legislation that focuses more on the needs of children, rather than the parents. Yet, "best interest" is a good example of how legislative change alone cannot change social attitudes and beliefs. Society and many courts, attorneys, and judges still believe mothers or female relatives are the best custodial caregivers for young children. This goes right to the heart of a mother's core belief; she is innately better suited to be the custodial parent and should control how the child is raised. She may believe that she is best qualified as the case manager for the children's care. Stereotypic parenting roles continue, not only within families but in society's expectations. Society perceives fathers as workers or providers, while mothers are the nurturing caretakers. Mothers in the workplace have dramatically increased in recent years. Many people do not believe that fathers are capable of nurturing in the same manner as a mother and, therefore, believe fathers cannot share parenting or have primary physical custody. Therapy must overcome these stereotypes that support irrational beliefs.

Irrational Belief: Fathers are not as capable as mothers to competently parent.

Parents and children display different degrees of resistance toward change. The difference between naive, active, and obsessed parents is their openness to look into themselves, see themselves for who they are, look past their defenses, and acknowledge the errors in thinking (cognitive distortions). Naive parents usually have a core belief that they are good parents and are willing to looking at their cognitive behavior and are receptive to correcting misinformation. The naive parent responds very well to education and has sufficient control to change his or her behavior. These parents will change their opinions when presented with reality. Core distortions are rarely an issue for naive alienators because they believe in themselves and are not threatened by the other parent's involvement with the children.

Much is the same for the parent who actively alienates. However, the active alienator is more defensive, struggles with guilt, and has little control over his or her behavior when triggered. They are amenable to education and learn from their past mistakes. They are willing to work on reconciling the identified realities, though not without an asserted effort. Typically, their distorted cognitive styles include: mental filtering, theorizing, and rejecting the positive, using emotional reasoning rather than rational reasoning, and catastrophic thinking.

The obsessed parent is a challenge for all because of the likelihood that he or she has a serious personality disorder or long-standing personality traits that resist change (Baker 2007, Eddy 2006, Summers and Summers 2006). The obsessed parent is quick to defend and will demonstrate black-and-white thinking, overgeneralization, mental filters, rejecting the positive, making assumptions, emotional reasoning, and catastrophic thinking. Treating an obsessed parent who has a personality disorder is difficult because they become more rigid and intolerant to change when stressed. They may require individual sessions to cope with the stress of working with the targeted parent. The targeted parent's face, voice, and even mannerisms may be enough to set off the obsessed parent.

Cognitive Styles

Cognitive styles are how an individual processes information. Rationalization, denial, black-and-white thinking, mental filtering, and emotional reasoning are examples of cognitive styles. The table below describes how distorted cognitive styles and core distortions contribute to the severity of the alienation.

The success of cognitive behavioral therapy (CBT) as a therapeutic modality for treating individuals and families lends support for treating high-conflict parents. I am drawing from CBT's success with many patient populations as a model for treating alienation. The treatment centers on the individual's irrational thoughts and cognitive styles that cause maladaptive responses to events. CBT lends itself well to helping high-conflict

Table 9.1. The degree to which distorted cognitive styles and core beliefs contribute to the severity of alienation

Alienator Types	Cognitive Styles	Core Distortions
Naive alienators	Mild	Not significant
Active alienators	Significant	Significant
Obsessed alienators	Severe	Very significant

parents identify and modify their irrational thoughts and beliefs that cause maladaptive parenting responses.

Change is painful. The therapist should acknowledge the pain, to the parents and children. For lasting change to occur, the parent must believe that any change made to protect and help the children adjust secures their belief that they are acting competently. Children must know that it is permissible to love and accept the targeted parent. Change must reinforce in the parent's mind that their core belief, "I am a good and protective parent" is strengthened now and for the future. They need to recognize their dysfunctional cognitive styles and adjust their thought processes without being blamed. Change will not occur if the parent feels humiliated, embarrassed, or accused of being a bad or abusive parent. The therapist can reinforce more positive or rational core beliefs. Both parents and the children must feel emotionally safe if change is to occur. The therapist can help lay the groundwork for change by complimenting and letting each parent know that the therapist sees his or her strengths as a parent. The therapist may be pleasantly surprised by the parent's reaction.

Exercise: Ex-spouse's Strengths

List three of your ex-spouse's strengths as a parent.

_____

_____

_____

Was this exercise difficult? You may have to set aside your anger to identify your ex-spouse's strengths. Remember, there was a time when you had positive feelings toward your ex-spouse. Now that you have purposely identified and listed the strengths, try making a point to tell your ex-spouse what you appreciate about their parenting style. Try to build his or her confidence. Stop making threats like, "I'm going to take you to court and get custody of the children." Threats only make matters worse and undermine any positives you tell him or her. By reinforcing the positive and eliminating overt negatives, in time, you may be surprised to see a change in attitude.

> Tip: Changing your thinking must include being open to the possibility that your beliefs and behavior contribute to the relationship problems.

Altering Obstacles to Change

Previous chapters discussed obstacles to change: symbolic communication, boundaries, blaming, parental and ex-spousal issues, and theorizing. The obstacles can diminish with education and discussion. Understanding symbolic communication helps the parent to empathize with what appears to be irrational emotions. Learning to recognize blame as a projection on others rather than taking personal responsibility offers hope for change. Discriminating between parental and ex-spousal issues protects the children from damaging arguments that are none of their business. Also learning to recognize theorizing as opposed to reality will prevent irrational behavior. The interventions are examples of what to say to help influence the parent's thinking. No single statement is going to fix the problem. The intervention is to help you understand the concept.

Interventions for Distorted Beliefs

The obstacles for change previously described are used to help your understanding of the relation between core beliefs, cognitive distortions, and cognitive styles. Below are actual statements made by parents embroiled in high conflict. With each obstacle for change are statements made by parents and examples of core beliefs, cognitive distortions, and cognitive styles. The purpose of the examples is to help you understand the differences so you can take time to think about your own beliefs and behavior. In the examples you will see a lot of overlap with the cognitive styles. Don't let that throw you. What is important is for you to understand what is meant by cognitive styles, so you can look at your own thought processes.

Boundaries

Frequent arguments between parents have to do with a change in boundaries. This often occurs before the final divorce. Boundaries are either written or unwritten rules about how a person should behave. Violation of boundaries can cause intense rage because a parent will feel violated. Frequently boundary issues can be resolved by educating the offender about the nature of boundaries, encouraging empathy, and acknowledging that there are new rules of conduct. The offender must be educated by the therapist in a way not humiliating but instead with empathic understanding about the new rules and how to behave.

Statement: "I can do whatever I want. You have to deal with it."

Cognitive Style: Emotional reasoning.

Core Belief: "I must always be in control."

Cognitive distortion: The reality is that a parent cannot do anything contrary to the law or court orders.

Intervention: During a separation or after the divorce, the reality is that the parent can do whatever they want with the children so long as what they are doing is legal, consistent with court orders, and the child's basic needs are attended too. "You have a right to express your feelings. That is not to say you have a right to control. Your being flexible helps reduce your child's stress."

Statement: "He always wants to know where I'm at."

Cognitive Style: Theorizing and overgeneralization.

Core Belief: "He wants to control me."

Cognitive Distortion: The reality is that a parent does not have the right to always know where the ex-spouse is located.

Intervention: The reality is that your ex-spouse has a right to his or her own life, personal privacy, and the right to come and go as he or she pleases. You could be accused of stalking if you consistently violate your ex-spouse's privacy. That includes your ex-spouse's time with the children. "Wanting to know if you left town is not the same as controlling you, though I can agree that you have a right to privacy. You should establish a boundary about what information is private, including your location." The therapist can firmly define reasonable boundaries.

Statement: "It's my house. I can come and go as I please."

Cognitive Style: Emotional reasoning.

Core Belief: "I'm not a bad person so why should I be rejected in this manner. I don't deserve this. I'm not a bad person."

Cognitive distortion: The reality is that after a divorce, the nonresident has no more right to access of the former residence than any other guest. He or she cannot enter the residence without an invitation.

Intervention: The offender needs to understand how the rules have changed since leaving the household. Continuing to walk into the house unannounced will be seen as offensive by the court and will cause your children to be frightened because of the confrontation. "You do not want to behave in a manner to cause your attorney to defend your behavior. On this issue, you will lose."

Statement: "No one is going to tell me when I can see my kids."

Cognitive Style: Dichotomous thinking and emotional reasoning.

Core Belief: "I'm a good parent. I won't hurt anyone. I don't deserve this treatment."

Cognitive Distortion: The reality is that the court can order when and under what conditions you will see your child. This is true for both the custodial and noncustodial parent. A parent must comply with a court order whether they like it or not.

Intervention: "You are a good parent, but forcing yourself on your children is not good parenting. Good parenting is reducing your children's anxiety and not exposing your children to what you believe is an injustice."

Core beliefs, or what we believe to be true about ourselves, can stir very strong emotional reactions when we think our beliefs are attacked. Trouble occurs when the targeted parent theorizes the other parent's motives for making the statement: "I know she said that just to hurt me." It may not be the other parent's intention to attack our core beliefs. A lot of misunderstanding is prevented if the two parents discuss changes in boundaries or the new rules that occur with divorce. This will require the parents to change their core beliefs.

Parental versus Ex-spousal Issues

Statement: "He is nothing but a sperm donor."

Cognitive Style: Emotional reasoning, rejecting the positive, and dichotomous thinking.

Core Belief: "I'm the only one who matters in my children's life."

Cognitive Distortion: The reality is that the law recognizes a father's right to have a relationship with the children unless you can show good cause to the court that would remove his parental rights because the decision would be in the children's best interest.

Intervention: "I know you are angry and hurt, but is it not true that your feelings reflect what he did to you and not what he did to your children? You may be very justified with your anger, but that is not the same for your child. Someday, do you think your child will want to make up his own mind about how he feels about his father? I have seen older children deeply resent a parent who prevents the children from deciding for themselves about the type of relationship they want with their father. Am I right that you don't want to be the object of your child's wrath?" You could be the object of your child's wrath if you persist in alienating the children. In time there is a lot that a father can contribute to the child's life. You do not have the right for your own selfish reasons to deny your child the opportunity to receive what a father has to offer.

Statement: "He never wanted my child. He wanted an abortion."

Cognitive Style: Emotional reasoning and overgeneralization.

Core Belief: "Rejecting me is rejecting my child."

Cognitive Distortion: It is irrational to think that a parent's feelings toward his child will not be different after he or she had the opportunity to bond.

Intervention: The reality is that parents' feelings change after they have had an opportunity to bond with the child. How he or she felt at the time of learning about the pregnancy may have nothing to do with how he or she feels today. The parent needs reminding that rejecting

---

her is not the same as rejecting the child. Frequently, a mother with this thought has an all-or-nothing attitude toward the biological father. She is probably dichotomizing her thinking, believing that he either loves or cares for her or he is absolutely useless. Her derogatory belief is in response to the pain that she feels from his rejection. In this day and age, it is not uncommon for both men and women to at least initially express the thought of having an abortion with an untimely pregnancy. If the biological father expresses this option and is subsequently rejected by the mother, the mother may hold this against him to rationalize her rejection and anger in response to his rejection. In effect, her distorted thinking, that he is incapable of caring about their child, helps to justify her continued rejection of the father. To restructure the mother's belief system, she has to first come to understand that an initial thought of abortion is not the same as deciding to have an abortion and, second, having the thought does not make either her or the father a bad person. "Maybe the father was just scared. Maybe she needs to empathize with the father's fear. Don't we all say things we later regret when scared or angry?" Therapists refer to a different way of looking at a belief as reframing an irrational belief to a more palatable belief.

Theorizing

Everyone at times is a mind reader. We make up in our mind what we do not understand. Sometimes we may believe that we know someone better than they know themselves. We read a facial gesture, listen to the tone of voice, or respond to their energy that fills the air. All these are cues ripe for a theory explaining someone's motivation for how they behave. The theory is likely wrong and becomes offensive when someone is telling you what you are feeling and motives for your behavior, as if they know better than you. Everyone has theories about why people behave the way they do.

Statement: "She won't tell me anything about what my children are doing."

Cognitive Style: Theorizing and emotional reasoning.

Core Belief: "She is keeping me from my children."

Intervention: The reality is that there is information that you can get about your children rather then depending on her. "I know your ex-spouse's behavior feels like you are being kept from your children. But you are hypothesizing. Let's see if together we can find out the truth." You need to sort out what information you have access to. An example is getting your child's hockey game schedule on the Internet or getting medical records from the pediatrician. In most states you do not need the others parent's permission to get copies of these records unless the court order specifically forbids you from getting the records.

Statement: "I know he just wants to hurt me."

Cognitive Style: Catastrophic thinking and emotional reasoning.

Core Belief: "I am helpless against verbal and physical threats."

Intervention: The reality is, if this is true, you can only change yourself and not depend on your ex-spouse changing. "You are sounding like you are weak and defenseless. We do not have control over how he behaves but you do have control over how you respond to him. We will help you find your strength rather than feeling like a helpless victim. Feeling helpless contributes to depression and low self-esteem."

Statement: "I know what is best for my child."

Cognitive Style: Overgeneralization and emotional reasoning.

Core Belief: "To maintain my competency as a parent, I must protect my child from the other parent's incompetence."

Cognitive Distortion: Fathers cannot possibly know as much as mothers about parenting because they did not give birth.

Intervention: The reality is that many fathers are very knowledgeable about parenting. Many of the books about parenting are written by males.

"Help me understand something. When you were married, were there times when the children's father took care of them? Did he discipline the children? Did he play with the children? Were you able to go to the store while father stayed home with the children? So what has changed? Is it possible that your anger and hurt is clouding your memories?"

Statement: "What am I to do? My son loves his stepfather and wants to use his last name."

Core Belief: "To be a good parent, I must always please my child. My child knows better than his father about what is best."

Cognitive Style: Rejecting the positive and emotional reasoning.

Intervention: The reality is that children should refer to the stepfather with a name or title that is most comfortable. Their wanting to call the stepfather "Dad" is more common for younger than older children. Older children may use the stepfather's first name. What is important is the child's comfort. Calling stepfather Dad doesn't have to be a threat to the biological dad so long as no one interferes with the relationship. What is equally important, and is considered alienation, is when a mother and stepfather coach the child to use Dad and refer to the biological parent by first name. That should never happen.

The parent needs to be educated about the legalities of name change and the consequence to the child, particularly if the father is or wants to be an active participant in the child's life. The mother must be told by the therapist in no uncertain terms that the child should not be allowed to use the stepfather's last name. Parents need to say no to their children. Mother in this example is ignoring the positive attributes that both father and stepfather provide. The implication in this example is Mother ignoring the importance of what the biological father has to give to their child.

Statement: "I am my son's father. My son should not call his step-father 'Dad.'"

Cognitive Style: Emotional reasoning and catastrophic thinking.

Core Belief: "If my child persists in calling his stepfather (stepmother) dad (mom), my child is rejecting me as a parent and I will lose my child's love."

Intervention: Parents need a little education and understanding of the child's perspective. Dad envisions losing his son's love if son persists in calling his stepfather Dad. This is catastrophic thinking because father is thinking the worse. The child's use of the terms Mom or Dad is very dependent upon the child's age. Young children and toddlers do not understand the biological definition of Mom or Dad. Instead they frequently use the word to signify the person or people that they perceive as important in their life and upbringing. Children rarely use the term with the intent of rejecting the biological parent. The therapist will help the parent to recognize the difference between using the word and the motivation or intent behind the use of the word. In effect, the parent is theorizing that the child intends to reject them as a parent if they call someone else Mom or Dad. Frequently older children, beyond puberty, will refer to a stepparent by their first name because they understand the biological significance of the term Mom or Dad. Sometimes when an older child is in the habit of referring to the stepparent as Mom or Dad, the biological parent will feel uncomfortable. Children have different reasons for calling a stepparent Mom or Dad. It is easier and the child doesn't feel that he has to explain the identity of the other male in his life. The other reality, though hard to accept, is when the child has a stronger bond with the stepparent. If this is true, father has work to do to strengthen the relationship rather than attacking the other family. Try letting the child use the title that is most comfortable for him or her.

Symbolic Communication

Symbols, perhaps unique to the parent and oftentimes not shared by the children or other parent, elicit emotional reasoning. The intensity of the triggered parent may be way out of proportion to the offense. Reasoning does not always calm the irrational parent. Someone trusted, usually not the ex-spouse, has to educate and try to reason with the irrational parent. Rather than challenging the parent's beliefs, education and helping the parent empathize with the children is less threatening.

Statement: "I won't let my daughter take her toys to her father's house because I will never see them again."

Cognitive Style: Catastrophic thinking and jumping to conclusions.

Core Belief: "To feel good about myself I must maintain control and power over my child's possessions. Her toys should be at her home."

Intervention: The reality is that children have a right to property. The toy is a symbol of who is in control and where home is. The parents need to understand that he or she is reacting to what the toy symbolizes. Does the intrinsic value of the toy justify the argument? Are there other choices about what to do with toys?

Stacy's Story

Stacy, a young mother of two, has been in and out of court trying to keep custody of her children. Though she is twenty-three, she acts like a seventeen-year-old. Because she loved to party (irrational behavior) and already had two citations for operating a motor vehicle while intoxicated, her mother gained temporary custody. Stacy was to appear in court to regain custody. Her children's father was also fighting for custody, arguing that Stacy was dangerous because she was cited for driving the children without a car seat (mother's irrational behavior). She frequently failed to appear in court, leaving her attorney standing alone defending his client's irrational behavior. Stacy argued that, "I have a life too and I am old enough to go out and have a couple of drinks (distortion). The court doesn't have a right to tell me how to raise my children (irrational belief, denying a reality). Fathers know nothing about caring for children (dichotomous thinking)."

Alcohol or drug abuse contributes to Stacy's cognitive distortions and her irrational behavior. Her cognitive style of overgeneralizing is a pattern of thinking that, in her mind, justifies her rejection of the biological father from parenting. Dichotomous thinking is damaging to the father's role and has nothing to do with drinking. Stacy is incapable of empathy and seeing beyond her own narcissism.

Cognitive Styles

Cognitive styles are how a parent receives, processes, and responds to information. We gather information from all our senses. We take that information, filter out what is believed to be relevant, give the information contextual meaning, and respond accordingly. During the stress of litigation and the threats to our core beliefs, the parent's cognitive style can become impaired. Bad habits in our thinking become more exaggerated. The thought process and the parent's behavior may appear more irrational. The cognitive styles described below are but a few of the many ways that individuals process information. The styles described are what are seen most often with parents involved in high-conflict litigation. The styles and examples described are intended for you to become more introspective and perhaps to better monitor what you have learned about irrational thinking.

Dichotomous Thinking

Dichotomous thinking, black-or-white thinking, or all-or-nothing thinking are the same concepts. The alienating parent may perceive the other parent's behavior as all good or all bad. There is no middle ground. This is especially true with severely alienated children. They may learn dichotomous thinking while learning to parrot their alienating parent. The parent will see themselves or others as a total failure if their behavior falls short of perfection. An example of black-and-white thinking would be, "I am a failure as a parent if I am not *always* there to protect my children." A more rational belief is, "Most of the time I am an effective parent and other times there is room for improvement." Parents as well as children need to be reminded to think about the gray areas in their life.

Exercise: Better Parenting

List three ways you can improve your parenting.

_____

_____

_____

Knowing you can improve your parenting skills does not make you an incompetent parent. I am sure there are aspects of your parenting that are very effective.

Overgeneralization

The parent sees a single negative event as a never-ending pattern of defeat. "He (she) will never change." Others may perceive the parent as overreacting. Kim is an example of how a parent overgeneralizes her belief that father is incompetent to care for a twenty-month-old toddler.

No one questioned that Kim is a loving and effective parent. Even her ex-husband admired her commitment to their children. Problems began when the father wanted to have their youngest daughter, Tracy (age twenty months), spend nights at his home. Kim vehemently refused, stating, "You can't have her overnight. What do you know about caring for a baby? You can't even change a diaper." The unstated core belief is, "I am a bad mother if I don't protect my baby."

These comments reflect an overgeneralization about fathers. The reality is that someone had to teach Kim how to change diapers, and a father is capable of learning. Mother encouraging and perhaps teaching father to change a diaper is protecting Tracy and reflects a loving parent who values the father's contribution to Tracy's upbringing. No one would argue that is a loving act.

Rejecting the Positive

Children also exhibit cognitive distortions, especially when alienated. They may reject positive experiences they had with the targeted parent. This is very confusing to the targeted parent because their experience is contrary to what the child reports. Alienated children have been known to say they have lied when they said they had a good time on vacation with the targeted parent. Part of the difficulty has to do with language development, particularly with younger children. Children are not developmentally mature enough to make finer discriminations like, "I am not in the mood." They use black-and-white or all-or-nothing thinking. Likewise, many adults reject positive experiences by insisting they "don't count" for some reason or another. Parents must remind themselves that gray areas exist in everyday experiences. They should guard against black-and-white or all-or-nothing thinking, and look for finer discriminations governing their decisions. Rather than saying "He is a poor excuse as a father," a more accurate statement is "Sometimes he doesn't know how to set limits on Jerry." Accusing a father as a Disneyland father is an example of rejecting the positive. "Jerry has fun with his father." Most importantly, parents must not reject the existence of a positive experience with their ex-spouse solely because of hurt or anger. There had to have been good times.

Jumping to Conclusions

Sometime in life, everyone uses this distorted way of thinking. With this cognitive distortion, the parent makes a negative interpretation of an event even though there are no facts supporting the conclusion. There are two types of this distortion.

- Theorizing: The parent arbitrarily makes a negative judgment about the motivations driving the other parent's behavior, without checking it out with the person. "If he really cared about the children, he wouldn't be spending all the money on bimbos every Friday night. He'd make time on Saturdays to see the kids instead of getting over another hangover."

- Assumptions: Similar to theorizing, this distortion in thinking relies on what a parent believes is fact when there is not supporting evidence. Parents accuse the other of lying without any evidence their assumption is true. This is an example of emotional reasoning. "I can tell by the look on her face that she is lying."

Emotional Reasoning

Another cognitive style that results in a cognitive distortion is assuming that a person's emotions reflect reality or facts. In other words, if it feels right, it must be right; "I feel angry because the other person did something wrong or deliberately hurt me." The parent ignores making intellectual judgments. "I just know that she is using the children against me. I can feel it."

A most serious example of emotional reasoning is "I know it is a matter of time before he will sexually abuse our daughter." This emotional reasoning leads to false allegations of sexual abuse that destroy families and the child that wears the stigma of being a victim when in fact the allegation is not true. You have learned that emotions are a very powerful motivator for how we behave and the outcome can appear to others as very irrational because the behavior is not grounded in reality. We need to listen to our emotions, but not by ignoring our rational judgment. There needs to be a balance between emotions and rational thought.

Catastrophic Thinking

This occurs when a parent exaggerates the importance or significance of an event. "If he really cared about the children, he wouldn't be fifteen minutes late." One way of overcoming catastrophic thinking is to put the event into a more realistic perspective by asking yourself to rate on a scale from 1 (not important) to 10 (extremely important) the gravity of the event. Stopping and asking yourself the question will slow down your emotional reaction. For the example above, you might rate the event as a 2, a nuisance but certainly not catastrophic.

Exercise: Catastrophic Thinking

You can do this exercise in your mind. Read each event and rate the importance or seriousness of each on a scale from 1 to 10

- Income tax audit
- Mowing the lawn
- Changing the day to pick up the children
- Deciding which restaurant to eat at tonight
- What to buy your aunt for Christmas
- What to wear tomorrow for work

Do you see the point of this exercise? This simple exercise really works. Putting issues in perspective helps to control our emotional reactions to events or thoughts. Taking time to think about the importance of an event delays an overreaction. The pause gives you time to think about how best to respond or what to say to the other parent and child.

Should, Must, Always, and Never Statements

Many parents set arbitrary requirements on their ex-spouse's behavior, without considering how their own distortions, motivations, and "should" statements affect the other parent. Mary accused her ex-spouse of being selfish because he bought a new car. She self-righteously stated, "He should not have bought that brand new car. If he cared at all about our kids, he *must* spend the money on them or put the money into savings for college. He *always* cares more for himself than his children." The connotation can also imply that he or she is a bad parent. "Joyce *should* stay home with our kids instead of dating. There's plenty of time for her to do that after the kids are grown." Avoiding "should" statements helps to reduce tension between the sender and the recipient because you remove the connotation of a demand rather than a request. No one likes being told what to do, especially by the ex-spouse. An alternative is to change the declarative statement to a question. "Do you think you could spend more time at home with our daughter?" Or "How do you think you are going to explain to our son about not having money for college when you buy a new fancy car?" The tone of voice is very important when asking these questions. You should be inquisitive and not confronting.

> Tip: Making demands on others can be offensive and can trigger a fight. Ask rather than demand someone to do something.

Practice Brings Change

Learning your cognitive styles will give you insight about how you process information. This takes considerable practice. Someone else may need to listen to your thought processes to identify your style because distorted thinking is a reflex that is often outside your awareness. The therapist will mirror your distorted thinking to help you hear your thinking, and help you learn a more rational thought process. Obsessed parents are going to have an extremely difficult time recognizing their distortions because the distorted thinking actually gets worse when the person is feeling challenged. Therapists must move slowly with these parents.

Self-monitoring

Self-monitoring is a very effective tool to bring about change. Parents are more conscious about changing their behavior if they pay attention to how they behave so they can make a conscious decision to change. The process begins with the therapist's educating you about the value of monitoring and then identifying the specific behaviors, thoughts, or cognitive style to monitor. The rationale is to replace the undesirable behavior with more desirable behavior. This occurs when the thought process changes. The parent must be able to visualize the behavior in question and agree to the value of changing the behavior. Together, the therapist and parent may rehearse the desirable behavior or dialogue.

Parents should understand how the specific behavior results in an undesirable consequence for them and the children. The therapist may ask you to write down on a tablet each occasion you engage in the new behavior and describe how the other person responds. You should only monitor a single activity, otherwise you will get overwhelmed. Self-monitoring can be very helpful for the parent wanting to learn more effective ways of controlling and expressing anger. Another example is asking the parent to monitor the number of times when he or she says positive statements to the children. The goal of the intervention is to increase the frequency of positive comments and to strengthen your parent-child bond.

Exercise: Monitoring

Identify a specific behavior you want to either increase or decrease. Get a little notebook and mark in the book or on a sheet of paper each time you engage in the behavior. This may sound corny but it works. Knowing you are marking the frequency will cause you to pause and think about how you behave. Over a few days, think about how you feel about changing your behavior and how people respond to you.

> Tip: Lasting change only occurs when you believe in the value of the change and your practice. This is true in sports, communication, and learning any new skill.

A Feedback Model

Therapists are trained observers. They listen to words, observe body language, and understand personalities and family dynamics that provide a framework for how to proceed in therapy. Admittedly, this is being simplistic. Therapists observe behaviors that you cannot see in yourself. They become your mirror. Learning more about yourself involves getting an accurate and unbiased assessment about how you behave. Feedback simply means that you are getting new information about yourself that you did not previously know. If you are already familiar with the information, that is not feedback. Being told that you are a "neat freak" when you already know you are compulsive is not feedback. Hearing from your child that "Daddy, you are always look mad," when you do not know that your child sees you as always angry, is feedback. A simple way of understanding feedback is learning three terms: specific behavior, nonjudgmental, and feelings. Learning to use these concepts while communicating will reduce hostilities, build your self-confidence, and promote greater cooperation.

Feedback is most effective when given with clarity, specificity, and sincerity. What inhibits good feedback is a lack of social skills and unrealistic expectations about the consequences of the feedback. Negative consequences are minimal when the receiver of the feedback is given effective feedback. Parents often say they don't want to give feedback because they do not want to hurt anyone's feelings. This is an irrational thought. If you stop and think about it, hurting someone's feelings is usually caused by how the sender communicates and less by the content of the message. If the sender is yelling, making accusations, and blaming, that is hurtful. Learning and practicing the feedback model will help avoid these problems and reduce your anxiety when knowing you are going to have an intense verbal exchange. The model is effective for both giving and receiving positive and negative feedback.

Being Specific about Behavior

Specific behaviors can literally be visualized in your mind. Pointing out specific behaviors does not tell the person to change (which people resent). Instead, it allows people to be responsible for their own behavior and the consequences. Then, they may choose whether to change their behavior if they clearly know what you are talking about. As well, naming specific behavior gives you greater impact and power when you give feedback, and gives the other person respect (nonspecific) and power when and if they choose to change. So, the person giving feedback and the one receiving feedback become more believable in their words and actions.

Here are some examples of specific behaviors:

- "You are thirty minutes late."
- "You are yelling at me."
- "I didn't get the report card."
- "I need to know the dates when the kids are out of school."
- "We must discuss our children's problems before making important decisions."

Do you notice that you can visualize each of these behaviors? In contrast, here are statements that are not specific:

- "You don't appreciate me."
- "I don't think you love your son."
- "You just don't understand me."
- "I can't stand you."

You will notice from these examples that you do not know what the sender is talking about. Being able to visualize the specific behaviors improves your understanding of what the other person is saying. This is not true with the nonspecific behaviors. How does a person behave who says that the other person is "appreciated?" The word "understanding" is another interesting word because it means the receiver can correctly repeat back what the sender is saying. If you listen carefully how the word is often used, the sender usually means that the receiver *agrees* with the sender's meaning. So, when you hear someone say, "Do you understand?" be careful how you respond because you may understand the person's message but not agree. If you do not agree, you need to say so. Nonspecific language forces the receiver to *theorize* about what the sender means. The receiver's theory may be wrong and can lead to serious misunderstanding, especially when the sender believed the message was clearly communicated.

Being Nonjudgmental

Feedback also must be given without judgment. Judgment implies good and bad or right and wrong. Most people fear judgment. Judgment can be offensive and can cause the receiver to get defensive and to counter-attack with blaming statements. Here are examples of judgmental statements:

- "You don't know what you are talking about" (right or wrong).
- "You're a bitch" (name calling).
- "You never listen to anyone. You think you are always right" (meaningless criticizing).
- "You don't know what it means to love your son" (meaningless criticizing).

Emphasizing Feelings

You may question, "What are you to say if you avoid judgmental statements?" The answer is: share your feelings. When you share feelings, use "I" statements and avoid "you" statements. "You" statements imply blame, causing the receiver to get defensive. One word describes feelings: angry, frustrated, happy, pleased, affectionate, sad, scared, nervous, etc. Here are some examples of the effective sharing of feelings:

- "Your yelling scares me."
- "I get frustrated when Sandy and I have to wait for an hour for you to pick her up."
- "I am more comfortable when you speak softly."

In contrast, here are some examples of ineffective communication:

- "The kids hate you!" (Judgmental, not specific thought).
- "The kids know you're a crazy, I have to agree with them" (Judgmental and not specific).
- "You are an inconsiderate bastard expecting me to wait." This statement is judgmental.
- "Shut your damn mouth" (This is a demand that is very offensive. The anger is there but this is not feedback).
- "Why should I listen to you? You don't respect whatever I say."

Learning the feedback model is not easy. It takes practice. At first using the model will feel very artificial. What is interesting about the model is its use as a diagnostic tool. If you listen to two people argue and apply the three words of the model, you can assess or conclude why the communication falls apart. Another important point is that the model applies for both receiving and giving feedback. For example, if you want to give feedback, plan and be sure that your message is specific. If you cannot come up with the specific behaviors, then do not expect the receiver to understand you. You need, first, to be specific about what you are going to say, before saying it.

Tip: Do not give feedback until you can identify and verbalize the specific behavior.

When you receive feedback, listen for the three components: specificity, nonjudgmental, and feelings. Although you cannot control another person's sincerity in giving feedback, most senders are *sincere*. Receivers subconsciously hear this sincerity even though their focus is on the message. If the sender's message is not *clear* and *specific*, ask the person to rephrase and to use *specifics* so you understand what the sender means.

Remember, understanding is not the same as agreeing. You may need to remind the sender of this fact. When the sender is name-calling or judging you, you can nicely ask them not to be judgmental and instead just to let you know how they feel about the specific behavior. This all takes practice but you will be surprised about the model's effectiveness. A good exercise is to listen to how the actors on soap operas use the model when arguing. They usually are very effective.

After learning the feedback model, you should begin practicing low-risk feedback and progressively work toward high-risk feedback about events or issues that you know could be problematic. Low-risk is giving your ex-spouse a compliment. High-risk might be giving specific and nonjudgmental feedback to a volatile ex-spouse or to an obsessed alienator. You should also be aware of the verbal and nonverbal response cues when giving feedback. Pay attention to your tone, your posture, and maintaining good eye contact, and keep your language brief and simple. The feedback model is rewarding because it helps you develop more self-confidence and self-control.

Spinning

One intervention with cognitive distortions is the ability of the therapist to offer the client a positive spin to their negativistic and catastrophic irrational belief. Spinning is the ability to rephrase a negative into a positive connotation. Metaphorically speaking, it is learning to see that the glass is half-full rather than half-empty. To use this technique, the therapist should be comfortable being a "spin doctor." Spinning is a form of reframing when the therapist enthusiastically offers the parent a different way of thinking about what is perceived as a negative event.

An example is the parent saying, "I am afraid to discipline my child because he gets angry and will tell his mother." The therapist, to the parent's surprise, will enthusiastically say, "Great! That means you are being an effective parent because your child's anger shows he respects you and your authority. He cares about what you say rather than apathetically ignoring you." The therapist emphasizes the point that the parent is effective and has much to offer his child, rather than feeling a failure and being intimidated by what the mother may think.

An effective reunification therapist would benefit from having the creativity and imagination to take negative self-statements and "spin them" into positive statements. The therapist must be able to see both sides of the picture. They should have the capacity to empathize with not only the children, but also the other parent's position. The therapist who just empathizes and reinforces a parent's irrational thinking risks failure, which damages not only the therapeutic relationship among all parties, but also prevents the irrational parent from learning and growing. Matters are also made worse because the therapist has over-identified with the parent or child thus losing his or her objectivity The therapist becomes an enabler who will destroy the trust of the other parent.

The importance of spinning is to help the parent modify their wording to a stream of thought grounded on reality rather than an irrational generalization. Words are important because they provoke emotional responses. As therapists spin negatives into positive statements, parents develop the ability to modify their own negative thoughts and words based on cognitive distortions to positive, meaningful, and reality-based self-talk and communications with the other parent.

Spinning can be fun for both the parent and the therapist. There is often a surprised look on the parent's face when they not only don't get the response they expect but now experience the challenge to the irrational thoughts. The parent starts seeing what the therapist is saying in a different light. This is progress.

Empathy Training

Both the alienating and the targeted parent usually have difficulty empathizing with the children and each other. This is because both can be self-absorbed being a victim or hating the targeted parent. Both will profess they are only concerned about the children, but how can that be true considering how some parents behave. Learning to empathize begins by recognizing the value of empathy, and by understanding what empathy means. A good example is flinching when your toddler falls and hits his head on the corner of the table. That is empathy.

Empathy training begins by learning how to recognize your child's feelings from statements, body posture, and their facial expressions. You are asked to put yourselves in your child's shoes and try to see and feel their world from their perspective. Stopping to observe the child's behavior and listening to what is said shifts the focus from the parent to the child. Then, the parent is instructed to consider how the child is feeling within the context of what is occurring around him. Taking time to describe what the child may be feeling is vital. Then, the parent should ask, rather than theorize, what he or she is feeling. Empathy involves taking time to listen to the other person instead of listening to yourself.

Coaching

There are times when a parent does not know how to talk with the ex-spouse or the children. Many parents mean well but have difficulty translating what they learn in therapy to the real world. Sometimes, the difficulty is the therapist being too abstract and the parent failing to understand the points made and how to apply them.

If this happens to you, ask for clarification or specific behavior. If you do not ask, you will not know what you are doing that is not working for you. You may need very specific instructions or coaching by the therapist about how to behave with the children or ex-spouse. Coaching involves you and the therapist first identifying a problematic behavior in a specific context. You should describe the context of the activity with as much detail as possible, in a manner so that the therapist can visualize the specific behaviors and interactions. You may be asked to role-play the activity so the therapist can observe what you are doing that is not working. This is referred to as getting baseline data. Notice I avoided using the word "wrong"; problematic interactions are behaviors that do not have the desired results.

After the therapist observes your behavior and language, the therapist will instruct you on alternative behaviors to practice. The therapist may instruct you on body language, your use of language, eye contact, and body posture. Therapists frequently refer to this technique as "assertiveness training." The therapist may ask you to again role-play but with the new behaviors. The therapist is shaping your behavior by giving you feedback as you repeat the process. With on-going feedback, your new behavior will be fine-tuned. Repetition helps to reduce anxiety. Examples of activities where coaching may be of help are: disciplining your children, saying no to your child, talking with your ex-spouse during visitation transfers, responding to criticism, and negotiating parenting time. You will probably be asked to practice assertiveness training in settings you identify as low risk.

Mental Imagery

Changing behavior is difficult, particularly in the heat of a battle. You may understand why you are doing what you are doing, but that is not enough to change destructive habits. Mental imagery is one easy-to-use method that improves the likelihood of successful change by rehearsing new behaviors, perhaps what you learned from assertiveness training (Libby, Shaeffer, Eiback, and Slemmer 2007).

You begin by identifying the specific behavior you wanted to change. Remember, specific means you can visualize the behavior. Then, with your eyes closed in a quiet space, visualize, with as much detail as possible, how you would like to behave. Visualize the room where this behavior is to take place, see the colors, listen for the sounds, see the person's face you are talking to. Then rehearse your words, visualize your body language, look the person in the eyes, with your back straight and your voice controlled. Don't worry about how the other person might respond. Instead, focus on how you are behaving. With practice and repetition in mental imagery, you improve the likelihood of engaging in your new behavior. You may also notice a change in your feelings when using the new behaviors.

Try these examples of mental imagery:

- Imagine going to vote, walking to the building, presenting your ID, signing the registration cards, and entering the voting booth. Think of the details in each scene. Picture the other people who you might see.

- Imagine what you would say to a co-worker who annoys you. Picture the details of your surroundings. Focus on the co-worker's face in your mental picture. Hear yourself speak the words you want to say. Remember the feedback model.

- Imagine receiving a call from a pushy telephone solicitor. Make a picture of where you are when you receive the call. Politely, but assertively, say "No" to the offer made. Hear your words and your tone of voice.

- Imagine your ex-spouse calling, asking to change parenting time for a special event.

After you mentally practice a few times what you want to say to your children or ex-spouse, see how you feel or respond when these situations arise. You may be pleasantly surprised. There are no guarantees of success, but you should notice improvement with both how you feel and how the other person responds.

Is It Time to Quit?

At some point, family focused reunification therapy should stop. Stopping should be considered if the therapy process itself becomes painful or damaging to the child's functioning. Therapy doesn't work for everyone all the time. Alienated children function fairly well for the most part. They are able to compartmentalize the access problems with other aspects of their lives. Most of these children can function quite well socially and academically. On the other hand, if the reunification therapy becomes stressful to the extent that grades fall and the child begins to appear depressed or socially withdrawn, there may have to be serious consideration given to discontinuing the therapy.

The therapist, with input from both parents and the children, should make the decision to terminate therapy. If this decision rests with the residential parent, there could be a risk that the residential parent may sabotage the therapy process, knowing they can manipulate the therapy and terminate treatment. Terminating therapy is difficult but with adequate planning, involving both parents and the therapist, termination need not be traumatic to the child. An emotionally fragile child may have to continue individual therapy with another therapist. The therapist should not be the reunification therapist.

> *Tip: Do not terminate therapy without first talking to the therapist. Not showing up or canceling late prevents the therapist from scheduling with another family.*

The ideal termination is when the family has reached the treatment goals. Often before termination, the frequency of the sessions is staggered out over time. When all agree, termination is appropriate, with the caveat that the therapist is available if there are future problems that cannot be resolved between the parents. There needs to be the agreement that either parent can ask the other parent to attend a session if needed.

Do not despair if you have not reached your ideal treatment goals. Instead, reflect on what progress you have made. Resist all-or-nothing thinking when judging success. If your child is feeling safe in your presence and is more accessible, you have had some success. Maybe there is greater tolerance between you and the other parent. That, too, is a degree of success.

Tying It All Together

You have learned different tools for change. Some tools will make more sense to you than others. You have to think about what you have learned and decide what is helpful. Practicing the different exercises will give you an idea what works for you. Now the issue is how to put what you have learned into practice.. Remember what has been emphasized throughout the book: changing feelings comes after changing behavior and/or thoughts. If you want change, look at your thought process, your beliefs, and ways to change your behavior. Consider the obstacles for change, the unyielding realities that you must reconcile, misinformation or cognitive distortions that must be clarified, and your cognitive style that leads to erroneous conclusions and irrational behavior. If you follow the steps for change and practice what you have learned, you may be pleasantly surprised by the results.

1. Identify and write on paper events that arouse strong feelings.

2. Identify your feelings. If angry, you may believe your rights or sense of fairness is violated. If depressed, you are struggling with a loss. Anxiety says you are threatened. If feeling guilty, you believe you did something wrong that needs to be righted. What do you think could explain your feelings?

3. Identify your core beliefs that threaten your esteem.

4. Identify the realities that you must accept and live with.

5. Identify your cognitive style that leads to irrational thoughts and dysfunctional behavior.

6. Write down your plan for change. The specifics of the plan would include many of the methods previously described.

7. Mentally rehearse the new plan for change.

8. Now take what you have learned and try to apply it when you think the timing is appropriate.

I know there is a lot to absorb in this chapter. If you gained just a little more insight, found a technique that makes sense and works to reduce alienation and tensions with your children, then I would call that success. You may have to study this chapter over again to reinforce what you have learned. You may have come to the realization that your role in changing your circumstance is a lot of work and more than just finding fault and looking for the other parent to change. Don't give the other parent all the power by you lying back and waiting for him or her to change. The fact is, you have to be part of the solution to negate the deleterious effects of alienation on you and your children.

Spontaneous Reunification

"I have given up. I see no hope in ever seeing my children again."

No one knows the number of parents who have given up all hope of ever seeing their children again. After years of trying to salvage a relationship, many parents feel beaten down, financially strapped, and angry for the court's failure to enforce court orders or to sanction the offending parent.

Desperate parents clinging to any remnant of hope sometimes behave outrageously, screaming comments to the estranged child or the other parent which they later regret. This was never truer than with the recent comments made by a well-known actor to his daughter, reportedly made public by his ex-wife. The father apologized for his verbal attacks toward his daughter. The public release of the audio tape called attention to the destructive effects of parental alienation. There was no excuse for calling his daughter a "fat pig." The father's desperation is only a glimmer of how thousands of parents feel. You may empathize with feelings of helplessness and frustration after being pushed away from your alienated child's affection.

In time, victimized parents begin questioning their motives for continuing the fight to have a relationship with their children. They seek counsel from others, asking if they should quit trying. Quitting is a personal decision at the heart of their core beliefs, a decision that only the parent can make for him- or herself.

Some parents are surprised, sometimes years later, when they abruptly hear from their alienated child. The child may now be an adult. Stunned, you are unsure how to respond. Perhaps you are as nervous as your child. You cautiously engage in conversation, knowing that saying the wrong thing could ruin the opportunity to mend the relationship.

Definition of Spontaneous Reunification

Spontaneous reunification occurs when the child *initiates* contact with the rejected parent without prodding, court orders, or forced therapy. However, a child's request for reunification with a rejected parent may be channeled through an officer of the court, a mental health professional, or a family member, such as a stepparent, a sibling, or even the identified alienating parent. The inquisitive adult or child may ask questions to others "in the know" if it is safe to reach out to the rejected parent.

> Tip: The child or adult child must feel safe from reprisal if they are going to reach out to the rejected parent.

Raymond's experience demonstrates the desperation a parent can feel after the court has restricted parenting time. His behavior in the counselor's office does not help his cause. After numerous court appearances, the court offered no hope of his having a relationship without the court's scrutiny.

Raymond's Story

Raymond, the father of an eleven-year-old daughter received the results of a psychological evaluation describing him as hostile to authority and mildly suspicious of others. Because of a prior hospitalization and a severe depression lasting two years, the court ordered Raymond to have supervised visits, one hour every two weeks. Raymond was angry. The report did not find Raymond depressed and later a psychiatrist ruled out clinical depression. Enraged, Raymond wadded up the report and threw it across the therapist's room, yelling obscenities and accusations. He knew he was losing control of his anger. He kept apologizing for his behavior, admitting during his rant that he was acting like the report describes. He repeatedly yelled his assertion that he had "no chance in the courts of ever being a father again. I'm a nothing to those people. I have no power."

Raymond's experience is similar to many parents who feel beaten down by what they collectively say is the "system" and the alienating parent. Their public display of their frustration and anger makes matters worse. The yelling and ranting reinforces the accuser's thoughts that they are right in restricting the child's access to the targeted parent. Raymond looked to the courts for answers and understanding but to no avail.

Many severely alienated parents will begin questioning themselves if their persistence only adds to their child's pain and risk of further estrangement. They question whether it is worth the tremendous legal cost, the frustration of seeing the court's failure to sanction a noncompliant parent, and the belief that the court perceives them as the impaired parent. Well-meaning friends and relatives often tender advice and support, telling him or her to, "Wait until the child is eighteen. One day your child will come to her senses and call." The well-intended counsel may soften the despair, but not for long. Holidays and birthdays are reminders of the loss. Yet, paradoxically, the rejected parent cannot afford to completely give up all hope for reunification.

The parent is not only losing a child but is losing the pride and social status of being a loving parent. Mothers can feel the social stigma of not having their child in their care. Fathers, though praised for their desire to be an active and loving father, feel persecuted by the system. Both feel the court's wrath caused by the adversarial judiciary. Both know that the system requires both parents to enter into the court arena and prepare for the attack. The court must sort out the attacks and separate truth from fiction before making a decision that can affect the children and parents for many years to come.

Tip: You must control your behavior in court. Misbehavior will be used against you.

When children are alienated or estranged from the rejected parent, both the parent and child must face the reality that the loss may be permanent. The court, using a mental health professional, may try to force reunification believing that reconciliation is in the child's best interest. Believing in reunification is understandable because family court officers and mental health professionals are in the business of hope. Many of these parents believe their only hope for a loving relationship with their children is to gain custody. Anything short of custody is unacceptable. There are many anecdotal examples where forced reunification and change of custody did break the stalemate, allowing a reciprocal relationship with both parents. The likelihood of a forced change of custody is remote for most alienated parents. Because there are no studies negating the potential damage to the child from a forced change of custody, courts rarely will take the risk of hurting the child by changing custody.

There are parents and children who have experienced successful reunification without any intervention from the court or by a mental health professional. Darnall and Steinberg (2008) learned from interviewing twenty-seven children (many now adults) and their parents how and under what circumstance spontaneous reunification occurred. Their anecdotal stories identified factors that contributed to successful reunification and explained why some reunifications failed. Also, knowing that spontaneous reunification can occur gives hope to soothe and comfort a parent's despair.

Parents and professionals alike want to know how to break the stalemate when a child wants nothing to do with the rejected parent. Intrinsic changes in the child or environmental events sometimes motivate change. The rejected parent may not be aware of these changes because the child will often keep their feelings to themselves until they find the courage to speak up. Ellie's story is an example of how a child's faith and maturity gave her the courage and motivation to reach out to her father after many years of being alienated.

Ellie's Story

Ellie is a rare young woman who had the courage to face her fears and reach out to her father after years of not speaking with him. She remembered her parents' divorce, which occurred when Ellie was only five years old. She does not remember who told her, but she came to believe that the divorce was caused by her father's numerous affairs with women from his congregation. Because he was the pastor of their church, her mother and Ellie's three sisters felt humiliated by his public affairs; the gossip hurt.

Ellie's mother admitted that she contributed to the alienation between Ellie and her father because of the betrayal she felt. When her husband left, she sought her children's emotional support. Ellie and her sisters became their mother's confidants during and after the divorce. Ellie in particular, her mother remembered, was extremely loyal, always trying to protect her feelings and meet her mother's emotional needs. She recalled subtle ways that she diverted the girls' esteem and affection away from their father.

Ellie remembers feeling angry and resentful toward her dad, especially after he married one of the many women with whom he had an affair. She remembered how devastated her mother felt when her parents' marriage failed. Even at a tender age Ellie knew her mother needed her more for support than her father did.

Ellie rejected her father's insistence that she accept his new wife as part of her family. She was appalled by the idea, believing that accepting this woman would be the ultimate act of betrayal to her mother. Ellie could not forgive her father for what he did to her family. So Ellie gave him an ultimatum, saying, "I don't want a relationship with you if you are going to have a relationship with her." Interestingly, Ellie later explained it was actually her older sister who threatened their father, ". . . and I just agreed with her." Father chose his new wife, and Ellie refused to see her dad for the next three to four years.

Ellie believes that the impact of her parents' behavior continued for her into adulthood, and even today there have been residual angry feelings that have emerged into her relationship with her husband. Ellie says, "I now have a very suspicious nature, even though I try not to. I have a hard time trusting people."

Early in her marriage, she explained, "I would go into fits of rage when my husband Bill wouldn't meet my expectations, or I thought he was cheating like my dad had done. Sometimes Bill's reassurance didn't help me. I would go into an emotional melt-down. I would feel better when he would hold me, and remind me that he was my husband, not my dad. I've always been afraid he would leave me, but he has reassured me that he would not."

Ellie's anger festered throughout her childhood and adolescence. She avoided her dad's phone calls because, "I felt terrible, like everything we lost was my fault. He made me nervous because I favored my mother." Like many children and young adults, it was easier avoiding confrontation than facing her pain.

However, throughout her life Ellie had been guided by her Christian beliefs and by her faith in God. At age fifteen during a prayer meeting for youth, she recalled a memory of herself as a four-year-old watching her father kiss a strange woman. Confused, she did not know if her memory was truth, or if it was part of her imagination.

She asked her mother about the memory because she did not understand its significance. Her mother told Ellie that the memory was true, and her reporting the incident led to the family scandal and the divorce. Even though Ellie cried bitterly over her memory, she reasoned that her faith helped her to recall the scene for a reason.

"I realized that God was trying to heal me and wanted me to have a relationship with my dad." Ellie came to understand, "I was alienating myself because I was afraid of my father's rejection." From her faith, she learned the power of forgiveness, "so I reached out to him, and began asking my dad questions about the past and about the disintegration of our family. Also, I would cry and tell him I needed him in my life."

Now Ellie says she has two fathers, her dad and her stepfather, as well as two mothers. Ellie was helped in reconciling with her father because he had the foresight to listen to what she said without becoming defensive or blaming. Her mother supported the reunification, putting her own hurtful memories aside and allowing Ellie to make her own decisions about what to do and say to her father. Mother rationalized that Ellie was old enough to decide for herself.

Though Ellie's experience with her parents' divorce is uncommon, there is much to learn from her experience years after the divorce. She, like many children of divorce, personalized her father's rejection of her mother, believing that somehow she was at fault for their separation. She further believed that any involvement with him was disloyal to her needy mother. Thus, she wanted to avoid all contact with her father who, in turn, blamed Ellie's mother for his daughter's rejection.

Tip: Do not use your children as your personal confidants or your therapist. Keep the boundaries of your role as a protective parent, and keep reminding yourself that your children are children and not little adults.

Ellie was a child victimized by both parental estrangement and parental alienation. Father's behavior estranged Ellie and her sisters because he personally and publicly abused the love and respect held for him by his wife and his daughters. He inflicted his own estrangement from his children because of his insistence that they accept his new wife as a family member before they were ready. Mother also contributed to the alienation by consciously or unconsciously communicating to the children that any forgiveness or acceptance of their father and his new wife was an added betrayal. The children shared her hurt and anger, making it too easy for them to reject their father and side with their mother. To cope, the children followed the adage: when uncomfortable, avoid. This was easy because father symbolized an unsafe and insecure parental figure.

Tip: Do not force or expect your child to warm up to your new partner before they are ready. Before introducing them or expecting them to share time with you and your new partner, your relationship with your child must be strong and without animosity.

During the time of her father's revelation, Ellie was at a stage in her development when she needed to rely on the safety and security of both parents. She sadly learned that she could not rely on her father. She recalled that her mother's family and older sisters harshly criticized her father in her presence. This caused Ellie to believe that she could not show any interest or affection toward her father if she were to keep her family's love and approval. She was afraid that she would lose them just as she had lost him. During the years that followed, Ellie knew that her mother was always there for her. The bond grew stronger. Quietly, she had questions about her father that festered but remained unanswered.

Tip: Do not expect your child to readily approve and accept your new significant other. Your child must set the pace for building the new relationship, not you.

For years, Ellie's father blamed her mother for alienating his daughters and sabotaging any hope for reconciliation. During the divorce and the many disclosures, he was not capable of accepting any responsibility for damaging the relationship with his daughters. He was unable to see his role in the destruction of the family. Sometimes, parents have the irrational belief that the nonoffending parent should somehow minimize the damage and protect them from the consequence of their misbehavior. They confuse their core belief (that they would never hurt anyone) with reality rather than taking personal responsibility.

Irrational Belief: When I have a problem with my child, I expect my spouse to stand by me and fix the problem.

Ellie's vignette has taught us that reunification can occur even under difficult circumstances. Stories such as Ellie's offer hope that spontaneous reunification can occur between the rejected parents and alienated or estranged children.

Rational Belief: I must take responsibility for my own behavior because I am the only one who can change me.

The rejected parent hoping for reunification has three considerations. First is not to give up hope. Second is how to prepare for eventual reunification, and third is how to respond when your child reaches out.

Darnall and Steinberg (2008) collected data for twenty-seven adult children who reached out to their rejected parents. Their stories give valuable insight about how reunification can occur. The children ranged in age from four to seventeen years when the relationship was severed. The length of time without contact with their rejected parent ranged from three months to nine years. The sample had fifteen males and twelve females. Nine were oldest siblings, five were middle children, and twelve were the youngest child. One was an only child. Three of the rejected parents were mothers and the remaining twenty-four were fathers.

The children's requests for reunification came from different avenues. Two initiated their requests through the minor's counsel (guardian *ad litem*) who previously represented them in court. Five channeled their request through a therapist, either their own or the therapist of their other parent; fourteen requested reunification through a family member, a stepparent, sibling or through the alienating parent. The remaining six children without assistance initiated the reunification by making direct contact with the rejected parent.

Success can take many forms, not just reconciliation but also a change in the parent's and child's beliefs or perceptions of each other. An example (see chapter 3) is Robert's realization that his father "is sometimes an ass, but I still care about him." Robert and his father may not have achieved a strong emotional bond, but both are satisfied that they can talk with each other and in a limited way be part of one another's lives. Some may not consider Robert's relationship with his father a success, but the son's favorable change in his perception of his father is not a failure for either of them.

There is a degree of crossover between the motivational models explaining the reasons for reunification. The reasons are not always definitive. A successful reunification was not always easy to assess because the length of time varied since the inception of reunification, and relationships tend to waver in intensity over time. The results from the follow-up of these cases found that one-third (nine of twenty-seven) had successful reunification, meaning there was a continuing, ongoing relationship between the child and both parents. Age was not a factor in predicting success. Also, by self-report these formerly alienated and/or estranged children indicated that they were satisfied with their parent-child relationship and felt accepted by each of their parents.

Tip: In all the cases, a crisis in the alienated child's life motivated reunification. A crisis is an opportunity for change.

Eighteen of the parents were not as successful with reunification. Nine children maintained some degree of contact with the rejected parent, but did not describe the relationship as "close." The remaining third said there was no further contact with the rejected parent for various reasons. The most common reason was the child's failure to see any reason to keep the relationship with the rejected parent alive. Any bond that previously existed was lost. After all the years of estrangement, it was easier to do nothing than work on the relationship. The rejected parent appeared to agree that the opportunity existed for continued contact if either desired.

Parents and children in the not-so-successful two-thirds portion of this sample suggested that reunification had limited success, because the rejected parent did not meet the child's expectations. The child did not believe that the parent really cared if the reunification was successful. Some of the children complained that the rejected parent only wanted to blame their other parent for past problems rather than focusing on how to improve their relationship. This made some of the children extremely uncomfortable. For them, it renewed old feelings of having to defend one parent against the other.

Several children reported that the alienating parent's persistence to destroy the relationship influenced their decision to end the relationship with their rejected parent. Even though their alienating parent had been initially supportive of the reunification, that acceptance stopped when the rejected parent once again became a significant person in the child's life. Therefore, the child felt obligated to return to the status quo of limiting or having no contact with the rejected parent. The risk of the alienating parent sabotaging the reunification does not always go away in time.

In two cases, two parent-child relationships continued to thrive, even though one parent kept trying to alienate. The alienating parent's attempts failed. Both younger adults were older so they were more independent, mature enough to sustain the relationships with each parent, and had the wisdom to keep these parent-child relationships mutually exclusive.

A lot was learned from these families about reunification though the sample size was small. In some of the less successful reunifications, the rejected parent lacked empathy, insisting on convincing the alienated child that their personal perspective about what occurred during the divorce was correct, and insisting the child's account was wrong. These parents continued to convey a punitive parenting style. A few of the rejected parents, who blamed their ex-spouses for their alienation, contributed to the estrangement of their children. Their inability to set aside their own emotional needs in deference to the child's needs, or their lack of knowledge about how to form an attachment, continued to feed the estrangement between them and their children. They could not tolerate the idea of being used by their child after many years of separation. Forming an attachment under these circumstances is very difficult and may require professional help. Some parents, at no fault to themselves, are just not warm and fuzzy parents but instead are cold and detached; these parents need help. They do not know how to bond.

Overt negative behaviors by the alienating parent ceased in order to support some of the child's initial reunification efforts, but the cessation was brief. The reunification proceeded slowly and in some cases stopped completely when the alienating behaviors resumed. However, for two children this did not adversely influence their renewed relationship with their rejected parent. For several others the intensity of the alienation caused the child to end the renewed relationship. As one fourteen-year-old described, "It was just too much hassle for me. Life was easier when I just stayed away."

Tip: The alienating parent's destructive tentacles can be relentless. Only the strongest child will survive providing the rejected parent does not blow it.

Parents and the children contribute to our understanding about reunification. The families had in common a rejected parent who had given up hope for reunification with an alienated or estranged child who no longer looked to the court for a solution. The alienating parent did not always support reunification, causing problems for the child. Crisis was the common denominator from the child's perspective. The crisis took many forms: ill health, the alienating parent's recent divorce, financial problems, and legal problems. Though there were varied degrees of success, we have learned that crisis can break a stalemate. History has many examples of how warring groups resolved hostilities when faced with a mutual threat. We all felt a unity or empathy after 9/11 and after the Florida and Katrina hurricanes. People come together after the crisis. Films like *Independence*

Day and *The Day the Earth Stood Still* develop this theme. After the crisis subsides, like in New Orleans, much of the passion for repairing the damage is lost because of a lack of interest. If one does not take advantage of the opportunity a crisis affords, the opportunity will be lost for another time.

There are anecdotal examples of judges creating a crisis in the courtroom to break a stalemate between two hostile parents. After learning the mother had coached their daughter to make false abuse allegations against the father, the judge created a crisis, wisely ordering both parents to jail (impending catastrophe). The father understood what the judge was doing. He was not bothered by the judge's action. After four hours, the parents returned to the courtroom for a reprimand. From that time forward the father had visits with his daughter. A second judge in Virginia recognized that the mother was hindering reunification, and the father was being obstinate. He ordered both attorneys to ask their clients for a name of two responsible adults to take custody of the children. The judge was not bluffing. He created a crisis for the parents. There was no argument or debate. Now the parents had to either work together or lose their child (impending catastrophe). A change of temporary custody was not necessary. The judge's actions taught us that creating a crisis could be a viable intervention for breaking a stalemate caused by severe alienation or estrangement.

Many of the problems that occur between a parent and child do not disappear because there is a crisis and attempts at reunification. A parent's long-standing personality problem or obnoxious behaviors can again raise dormant issues for the child and spawn anxiety over the connection that was wrongly identified as alienation. For many parents and children, reunification therapy may prove helpful if the parents and children cannot overcome these obstacles. Many of these families went on with their lives with a new unity without professional or court intervention.

Preparing for Spontaneous Reunification

There are ways that rejected parents can prepare for a possible reunification. Though a parent may have given up hope, the rejected parent can improve their chances of reunification if they:

- Maintain self-control over what you say to your child and the other parent. Be careful what you write, text message, or e-mail. What you write can be held against you. Do not retaliate with your own alienating behavior.

- Always try to know the location of your child.

- The child should always know how to find you by keeping your attorney or family members informed of your whereabouts and doing your best to keep web site, social-networking site (such as MySpace or Facebook), or your e-mail addresses updated.

- Always acknowledge holidays. Your child may ignore or never receive your gifts. The gifts may be returned. What you do not know is if your child or the alienated parent returned the gifts. Do not jump to conclusions. Later your child may ask why you did not acknowledge holidays. Holidays are very symbolic of caring and love. An obsessed parent frequently tells severely alienated children that you did not love them, or you have no interest in them. That is why you were not part of their life. You do not want to lie to your child but instead show him or her gifts or cards that were returned and saved. After all, the mail and gifts are not yours.

Tip: Save all mail or gifts returned. Someday you may want to return the mail or gifts in person.

- Avoid unloading your anger on your child. After all, they are also a victim.

- Your goal in communicating with your child is to reduce their anxiety. If your child is going to reach out, they must feel safe. Sometimes parents ask what they should do in a particular situation. The answer is whatever reduces your son's or daughter's anxiety.

Responding to Spontaneous Reunification

How you respond when you get that call can be the difference between success and failure. You must be patient and listen well before reacting. Try to be soft spoken, letting your son or daughter know that you are glad to hear from them. Keep in the back of your mind that your son or daughter could be calling because they are in a crisis and need something from you. Sometimes parents will ask, "How do I respond?" The answer is simple: say whatever you believe will reduce your child's anxiety. Be prepared for your child to ask for something that causes you to feel used. He or she may ask for money for school or a car, help with a legal problem, or whatever his or her needs are in the moment. Do not abruptly answer without first thinking about what to say. You may have to decide if you are comfortable feeling used after years of being alienated and perhaps degraded. Most parents successfully reunified are comfortable making this decision.

One way of destroying any chance for repairing the damaged relationship is insisting that your children hear your side of the story, expecting him or her to agree with your memories about what occurred. Most alienated children, even as adults, have very different memories. As hard as you try, their memories will not agree with yours, especially if most of the alienation occurred when they were very young. The harder you try to convince the child you were right, the more you will push them away.

Many alienated children do not want to talk about what happened to cause the years of separation. Sometimes your child may feel guilty for not reaching out, fearing that you are angry. He or she may want to hear that you are glad to hear from him and are not angry. You should respect their wish to avoid certain questions and topics. If your child inquires about what happened, take your time to respond, and think about what you are going to say before speaking. Whatever you do, do not retaliate against the other parent with blame and your own alienating comments. Suggesting that the years apart are "your mother's (father's) fault" is not something your child wants to hear. Such statements are a sure way of pushing your son or daughter away again. When answering their questions, answer as you would answer questions to your children about sex. Be honest, brief, and do not overly elaborate.

Irrational Belief: If I can explain to my child about what happened that caused the alienation, he or she cannot help but agree with my argument.

It is critical how you respond to your child's reaching out. Keep in mind the following ideas that should help you succeed. Knowing what not to do is easier than knowing what to do for repairing the relationship. You must be patient.

- Spontaneous reunification can occur anytime. Be prepared.
- When not knowing what to do or say to your alienated child, the best answer is to do or say what will reduce your child's anxiety.
- Do not retaliate against the other parent with your own alienating behaviors or comments.
- Expect to feel used if you hope for spontaneous reunification.
- Do not force any commitments. Move slowly, allowing your child to set the pace.

- Be enthusiastic, but control your passion. Do not overwhelm your child with your excitement.

- End the conversation on a positive note.

Rational Belief: My child's experiences are different from mine. Consequently, he or she may have different memories about the alienation. My child may never agree with my beliefs and memories.

Spontaneous reunification is always possible, even after years of hopelessness. Try not to give up hope. Prepare yourself for the possibility. At the same time, go on with your life. If you obsess about the injustice of losing your child, consider getting professional help.

Other Issues

You probably realize by now the many issues and questions that come up during the course of litigation. This book is not a comprehensive resource on divorce. There are other excellent resources available. However, there are issues frequently raised that are related to alienation that are addressed below.

Refusing Parenting Time

Perhaps the most common complaint that raises the allegation of parental alienation is the parent's refusal or child's refusal to visit. Do not jump to conclusions by thinking the worse. This is a very complex issue, because there are many possible reasons other than alienation as to why a child does not want to visit. What you do not want to do is get into a confrontation with either your children or ex-spouse by getting into a blaming and yelling match in front of your children. It is not always your ex-spouse's fault that your children are not wanting to visit.

Older children sometimes do not want to visit because they see some other activity as being more fun and exciting. They will be more inclined to visit if they know that they can have the same fun activity while in your care that they would have by staying home. When raising teenagers, especially if they are socially active, they will judge where they are going to have the most fun. Don't get into the trap of trying to compete with your child's friends for their affection and loyalty; you are likely to lose. Your child wanting to be with their friends is not meant to hurt you or say, "You are not important."

You may want to consider the suggestions below if you want to try to prevent problems with parenting time.

- Do not fight or argue with your ex in front of your children during the exchange. Children and teens should feel relaxed during the exchange.

- Make it a point that your child is feeling good about you when they leave.

- Don't end your parenting time with your child believing you are angry. Always make up with your child an hour or two before the exchange. Children will often judge the time spent with you by what happened in the last hour. They will remember those feelings until the next parenting time. Your child will not want to return if they believe you are angry with them.

- Common sense (as well as research) will tell you that people, including children, like to be with people who make them feel good about themselves. If the majority of time spent with your children is punitive or stirs negative feelings, they will not want to spend time with you. If this is a problem, you need to make it a point to spend time together that is more positive. Be nurturing and caring rather then critical and punitive. Children want to hear you brag to others about their accomplishments, gloat over their successes, and hear your praises. On balance, there needs to be a greater amount of praise rather than criticism to strengthen your relationship.

When Are Babies and Infants Old Enough to Spend the Night with Father?

I realize this question is sexist but I think there is a gender preference for who is able to care for a baby or infant. This is a difficult question to answer because the answer is more theoretical than grounded on research. There appears to be a consensus that believes children under the age of three require a consistent and stable environment that allows the bonding with a primary caretaker, the custodial parent. The statement is interpreted to mean that a baby or toddler should not stay overnight with the noncustodial parent. Noncustodial parents, usually fathers, will question why the child is not able to bond with both parents rather than one parent at the exclusion of the other parent. There is no simple answer. How a child adjusts to transitions and changes while staying overnight depends a lot on the child's temperament and the quality of the parents' relationship. When parents are able to peacefully work together, overnight visits are less of an issue. Both parents, including the noncustodial parent, have to accept that what is best for the child's adjustment comes before your sense of entitlement.

If you and your ex-spouse are unable to come to a mutual decision about overnight parenting time, the court will do it for you. I realize that I am not answering the question. Personally, I know of no studies concluding that infant or toddler overnight visits with the noncustodial parent are damaging, though there is developmental theory that would question the practice. Many infants and toddlers spend overnights with grandmothers without questioning any harm to the child. That is why I wonder if the issue is decided by a gender bias. No one questions that children are able to bond with both parents in intact families.

Overnight visits with babies and toddlers are only part of the problem with parenting time. Most court orders will allocate parenting time based on the children's current ages and developmental levels. The orders do not take into consideration changes in the child's temperament, developmental needs, or even if the child is impaired. The expectation is that the parents will work out these issues between themselves taking into consideration the children's needs and wants. The assumption is that the parents will recognize what is best for the children and defer their own needs and wants. This sounds great in a perfect world without alienation. Unless the court says otherwise, children have no choice but to visit and the decision is not theirs to make. Effective parents must not be selfish. If you believe that your ex-spouse has a sinister motive to chronically restrict your access, talk to your attorney about your options. Do not keep arguing with your ex-spouse if you are getting nowhere. You will just cause more damage.

Gay Relationships

Learning that one parent is gay is becoming more common. Hearing the disclosure still causes many courts and parents to feel very anxious about custody or parenting time because of not knowing what effect a gay parent has on the children. Some parents fear that an openly gay lifestyle is contagious and will influence their children's sexual orientation. There is no evidence to support this claim. Other parents fear that a gay lifestyle promotes promiscuity. Again, there is no evidence to support this assertion. Gay parents like heterosexual parents are expected to behave like any other parent. Children should not be exposed to sexually inappropriate behavior, overly demonstrative affection with the significant other, or any behavior that causes the child to feel embarrassed or uncomfortable. The children's best interest to have a mutually loving relationship with both parents must come before any political or social statement. Gould, Martindale, and Eidman (2007) expressed the opinion after reviewing the scientific research that parental sexual orientation, by itself, is not a factor that adversely affects children's best psychological interest. Homosexuality, per se, has not been found to harm the child's adjustment or to influence their sexual orientation.

Threatening Violence

"I'm going to kick your ass if I find out you lied to me."

There is a disturbing increase in family violence with today's divorces. The risk of violence is greater after the separation and the divorce. When there is a history of domestic violence, you should not be lulled into complacency after the divorce or separation. Husbands and wives seem to have less control over their behavior. They act impulsively with little thought about how their behavior harms themselves or the children. After regaining control, the parent may feel embarrassed or remorseful. The violence may surprise everyone, including the offender. There are many occasions when the offender has had no previous history of domestic violence. Unfortunately the stress from deciding on the divorce and the accusations and counter-accusations can be too much for some parents to tolerate without losing control of their anger. Parents sometime have to know when to walk away and regain self-control.

After the divorce, the victimized parent cannot assume that the offender will offend again. A single violent act is reason to be cautious but does not mean that future violence is inevitable. Although the common view today is to believe that once you offend you will always be an offender, this is not supported by research.

Violence is likely to recur if the offender assumes no responsibility for his or her behavior but instead blames others, giving the perpetrator reason to justify future violence while offering no incentive to change. Alcohol and drug abuse are another risk factor. A professional rather than an ex-spouse should assess a parent's potential for violence. In all fairness, even professionals do poorly in predicting violence. The individual's history of previous violence and their abuse of alcohol or drugs are the best predictors of future violence. Psychologists can only assess a person's personality and mental health and provide some insight into potential violence.

A victimized spouse sometimes uses his or her experience with the ex-spouse to boost arguments to prevent parenting time (or visitation).

Professionals and the courts must be cautious before taking away a parent's right to visit because of a past violent incident, however. The argument "He abused me, so it's only a matter of time until he will abuse my son" does not hold water without looking at the perpetrator's history. Fearing violence because of your ex-spouse's past treatment toward you does not always justify stopping parenting time without a court order or a recommendation from your attorney. Though there is reason to be concerned, you cannot assume your child will be abused or assaulted. If you are physically assaulted, you should report the incident to the authorities and your attorney. Many times the abuser will do everything in his or her power to keep the assaults secret. This is how the perpetrator attempts to control you. The irony is that making the abuse public will more likely help the perpetrator maintain self-control. Do not jump to conclusions and make false allegations. Recognize there are different opinions about what constitutes abuse. Not everyone will agree with your assertion. A conclusion in the court that abuse occurred takes more than your word. The perpetrator will likely deny your allegation. Remember that a police report is only an account of what was reported and observed and not necessarily evidence that abuse occurred. It is up to the court to make that conclusion.

> Tip: Perpetrators, knowing that the world is watching how they behave, are more likely to maintain self-control.

A word of caution to the parent who has or is prone to assault. In many, if not most jurisdictions, a conviction for domestic violence will just about eliminate any chance of you getting custody and perhaps unsupervised parenting time. This is why false allegations by an alienating parent are a threat. Parents obsessed know how to stop the targeted parent in their tracks with false allegations. Be careful and strive to keep strong your relationship with your child and to contain your behavior.

In recent years, women have reportedly become more aggressive. Many have been known to attack their husbands and cause serious injury. Weapons are a tremendous equalizer when a woman assaults a man. Even when the woman is clearly the aggressor, it is still the man who frequently gets charged with domestic violence though this trend is changing. This is true for a couple of reasons. First, men still feel embarrassed that their wives have assaulted them. They may think it's degrading to report the assault to the police. Second, the person who gets charged with the assault is usually the second person who gets to the police. Men take too long thinking about what to do while their wives are faster getting on the phone.

After years of living with your spouse, you learn the vulnerable spots in each other's armor. You know what to say or do that will drive your spouse crazy. When the marriage was good, spouses trusted that their partner would not push those buttons. When the marriage falls apart and there is a loss of power, a spouse may react by pushing buttons to equalize their advantage. One spouse may accuse the other of being fat, being a lousy sex partner, never having time for the family, etc. Whatever the accusation, it sets off a fury of hurt and rage and perhaps a threat of violence. If violence erupts, everyone may feel guilty and scared afterward, particularly the children. Someone probably needs therapy.

Exercise: Keep Your Fingers Off Those Hot Buttons!

After having been separated or divorced for a time, it is easy to forget those little digs or criticisms that drove your ex-spouse crazy. This exercise will help remind you of those criticisms that trigger your ex-spouse's hurt and rage. Take a few moments and remember back to the arguments you had. Think about what triggered the argument. If you are having trouble remembering, think back to the topics or comments you avoided to prevent a fight. Make a list of the comments below.

1. _____
2. _____
3. _____
4. _____
5. _____

It is likely that any of the things you have just listed can still trigger a fight between you and your ex-spouse. If you want peace and cooperation, do not push these buttons.. If you push any of these hot buttons, you can be assured you are going to be the loser. Remember, you have your own hot buttons that can also be pushed.

Managing Grief

Any loss causes grief. First, know that you are not alone. There are others, both mothers and fathers, who have similar experiences, and who are in deep agony over the loss of contact and meaningful relationship with their children. This goes for grandparents too.

Second, know that you are not crazy. In our culture we are not encouraged to publicly express our grief. We are taught to be strong, rise above it, tough it out, get over it, and get on with life. Sometimes that is wise counsel if we linger in our pain, and our outrage becomes the complete focus of our life affecting our work, our social life, and our spirit. However, the loss of a child whether by death or by exclusion from that child's life is beyond the realm of many parents' ability to cope.

In the beginning of an alienation cycle parents may struggle with wanting to deny that the person they once loved and trusted would threaten to exclude them from their child's life. Denial is the strongest emotional defense we have at our disposal, and it is the defense that we rely on the most, especially during the beginnings of the divorce. For most parents, because they truly want a relationship with their child, their denial of the ex-spouse's intentions does not hold up under the scrutiny of time or the emotional disconnect they experience. With the passage of time and continued refusals from your children, the denial turns to anger and rage. Now the battle lines are drawn and the time with the children becomes the bounty.

Denial and lack of understanding of parental alienation causes the parent to delay getting legal help to fight aggressively to get their parenting time restored. The more time that passes before taking action, the more difficult to successfully intervene. When you start to see a pattern of alienation and refusals to visit, it is imperative to get legal counsel immediately.

Third, many parents are confused about how to cope with the different feelings. You may experience deep sadness, intense anger, extreme outrage, and desperate blame. To keep from being overwhelmed by this internal "bucket of worms," many parents try to detach from the situation, believing this is an act of self-preservation. Some bargain using the following logic, "My child will understand what's happened when he/she turns eighteen so I'll just wait." Both strategies are akin to whistling in the dark.

Fourth, targeted parents want to know how to deal with these strong emotions in healthy ways because, if allowed to remain unreleased, they often gain a life of their own and emerge at inappropriate and inopportune times toward others who do not understand or deserve the depth and intensity of the feeling. Sometimes emotions are held inside. In an attempt to self-medicate pain and kill the pain, the targeted parent turns to addictive behaviors or substances. Eventually, if strong emotions are held internally for an extended time, they can bring about physical problems that can plague the individual for many years to come.

So the dilemma remains: what do I do with my grief and pain? Keeping a journal or diary is helpful, but strong emotions require active self-interventions. Having a good cry or a private scream may give you a little relief from your hurt. Don't be embarrassed expressing your grief during your private moments. It may also be helpful to take a sequence of your child's pictures so you can activate your feelings of loss. Remember, the depth of your sadness reflects the depth of your love. The price we pay for loving someone is the risk of being hurt. Would you have it any other way, that is, to not love to avoid hurt?

Having a physical outlet helps to temporarily dissipate anger or distract you from your depression. Bowling, driving golf balls at a range, jogging, or exercise will give you a respite from your anger. True, your hurt or anger will raise its ugly head after the activity is over but the distraction reminds you that you have some self-control of your feelings. The relief from the activity doesn't remove the grief or make the issues go away. What is worse is doing nothing but obsessing over the betrayal and reasons for your hurt.

Outrage describes the parent who feels misunderstood or not listened to. They need supportive attention from someone willing to hear their story. This is why parents find court is so frustrating. Parents are shuttled into a little room, waiting for the attorneys and judge make major decisions affecting their lives and their children's lives without any opportunity to tell their story. They know after the decisions are made, the attorneys and judge will go home and sleep well that night while what is left of the family goes home and agonizes about what occurred at court. The problem is finding a receptive listener who has the patience and energy to hear the saga of hurt, frustration, and humiliation more than once. Targeted parents can tell their story into a small tape recorder, share their story with a trusted confidant, or write their story in a journal. Many parents have told me they were going to write a book about their experience, saying that more parents need to be aware of parental alienation. Some parents have successfully published.

What is important is to ease the outrage if the court's decision implies that you are less important, or nonessential, in your child's life. It is important that you are heard, and that you remind yourself that you are still a parent by keeping your child's pictures around you and acknowledging the children's holidays. Another approach is to involve yourself in the parenting role with other children as a godparent, as an involved uncle or aunt, or a Big Brother or Big Sister. Validating yourself as a parent can go a long way toward healing feelings of outrage, though the memories don't go away.

Finally, desperate blame is probably the most difficult bereavement issue to process. Some blame is justifiable but do not let it destroy your spirit. Becoming obsessed with revenge will destroy the quality of your life and will not reconcile the issues with your children.

Should You Give Up?

This is never an easy question to answer. I encourage parents not to give up but if they do, there is a right and wrong way to go about quitting. There is the risk that giving up can lead to your never seeing your child again. No one can guarantee that years later your child will see the light. Spontaneous reunification does happen. Supportive friends may say, "Just wait, your child will come to his senses." That sounds nice but do not assume that is true. I do not know of any statistics about reunification but my guess is that most often it does not happen, especially when the child/adult is victimized by an obsessed parent who has no ability to see the harm they have caused their child.

Healing from your loss is not easy and never will be easy. Your mind may struggle between trying to talk yourself into not caring to the other extreme, fantasizing how you are going to get back at the other parent. Revenge rooted in anger and hurt does not work for either giving you peace of mind or getting your child back. At this point, you have a big decision to make about how to proceed—a decision that can affect how you and your children will feel for years to come. If you decide to quit, consider the following advice.

- Do not be vengeful.
- Talk to trusted friends, family, and your attorney before making the decision to quit.
- Make your decision when you have control over your feelings.
- Then, communicate your intentions to your ex-spouse and children in person if possible. You may consider having someone your child trusts to sit in. I have had parents record their intentions on video for their children to watch. They give one copy of the video to the child and keep another copy in case the original is lost or destroyed. The attorney or counselor can arrange for the viewing so the children can talk about their feelings after watching the tape.

Children, like adults, need to talk out how they feel with someone whom they trust and who has experience talking to distressed children.

- Always be civil when talking with your children and the other parent. Share your love not your anger.

- Explain to your child that you are not angry and will always be available.

- There is always the possibility of a spontaneous reunification. For this to happen, your child must always have a way to contact you. You should have available a web site, an e-mail address, cell phone number, or a social-networking web site (MySpace or Facebook, for example) for them to contact you. Let your child know how he or she can always find you and that you will be thrilled to hear from them.

- Expect to continue paying child support. You cannot rationalize not paying support because you are not seeing your children. From the court's perspective, the two issues have nothing to do with each other.

- Continue acknowledging significant dates like birthdays and holidays with cards and gifts. Save the gifts and cards for later if returned unopened. Gifts are very symbolic of love. Years later your child may ask, "Why didn't you sent me a birthday or Christmas present?" You are better off being able to say, "I did. They were returned but I still have them for you." Saying nothing only reinforces in your child's mind that you don't care.

Some parents become socially active for social change. Many parents have asked how they can become more involved in letting people know about parental alienation and parental alienation syndrome. There are many parent advocacy groups that offer support and a constructive way of directing your hurt and frustration with the system. Continuing to blame and complain may do little to resolve your feelings or help your case but at least you will feel less helpless and less isolated.

For your sake and the sake of your relationship with your child, it is imperative that you find a place in your heart to forgive the other parent. Forgiveness and not retribution is the only way of finding peace and moving on without that occasional knot in your stomach. Some parents argue that their ex-spouse does not deserve forgiveness. What you may not understand is that forgiveness is for *you*, not the ex-spouse. This is not to say that you will forget all that has happened. You won't. For some people, this is a spiritual journey, and for others the path is a secular one. What is important is that you go about this process in a unique way that you believe will work for you so the specter of losing your child is diminished, and your health and well-being are restored.

Relocation

Relocation is a difficult issue, especially if a parent remarries, has an out-of-town job offer, or wants to return to a community where they have more family support. Stahl (1999) wrote that "for the child custody evaluator, move-away cases are among the most difficult and emotionally sensitive, often because there is no middle ground that can reduce the conflict or potential risks to the child." Most jurisdictions have specific requirements that must be met before a parent receives the court's permission to move. The criteria could be the distance of the move or if the move is out of state. There are cases when a parent moved out of state without the court's permission and later was ordered to return to the home state. This can and does happen, so do not be presumptuous to think this cannot happen to you. Always talk to your attorney before making any significant moves that could be interpreted to exclude or restrict the other parent's parenting time. The other parent may decide to seek a change of custody to keep the children in their familiar community.

The court's primary concern is the child's best interest and that includes maintaining a relationship with both parents. For these reasons, courts want to know the motivations for the move and what are the parent's plans for assuring that the children maintain a strong and healthy relationship with the distant parent. The other issue taken into consideration before a decision is made is the child's feelings about the move and the relationship with both parents. There are claims (Wallerstein and Tanke 1996) that maintaining a loving and nurturing relationship with the custodial parent has to take priority over the noncustodial parent's rights. They also claim that a positive relationship with the custodial parent has a greater influence on the child's overall adjustment than the relationship with the noncustodial parent. This makes sense when the majority of the children's time is spent with the custodial parent. This can be hard to swallow for the noncustodial parent who feels relegated to a less significant status in their child's life. The noncustodial parent may allege that the motivation for the move is nothing more than the custodial parent's desire to alienate and control. He or she may argue that the move will not benefit the children and instead harm the children because they are being removed from a loving and stable environment. These may be good arguments, but it is the judge's call. There are no easy answers other than presenting your arguments before the court and not exposing your children to your anger and bitterness.

Abduction

Abduction is a very complex issue because there are times when there is no agreement as to what is an abduction. Typically abduction is seen as an intentional removal of the child from their residence and familiar surroundings without the other parent's permission or knowledge of the child's location. Kidnapping has been defined (Hoff 1997) as ". . . taking, retention, or concealment of a child by a parent, other family member, or their agent." Any way you look at it, abduction or kidnapping, the result is a damaged child who will forever hold the memories. The child's relationship with both parents may never be the same.

There are many reasons why a parent would abduct a child.

- A fear of losing custody or access to the children.
- A belief that the parent is protecting the child from a perceived threat of abuse.
- A desire to punish the other parent.
- To create leverage to reconcile.

There is a risk of abduction when:

- The parent threatens abduction or has abducted in the past. The risk of reabduction is very high.
- A history of alienating behavior such as denigrating comments about how the other parent has no value to the child.
- A parent has no regard for the legal system. To take such a drastic action as abduction or kidnapping shows no regard for the legal or social consequences.
- The parent or child has joint citizenship in another country.
- The parent or child has relatives overseas or in another part of the country.

- The parent is extremely paranoid, suggesting to the children and others that their safety is at risk if they remain at their current residence.
- The parent has a prior criminal record.
- The parent is unemployed or has very few ties to the community.

Abduction is alienation in its most severe form because the parent has to brainwash the child to rationalize the abduction to the child. Abducted children have to be made to believe that the other parent either no longer loves them, is a threat to their safety, or is undeserving. Sometimes the abducted child is given a new identity or is reprogrammed with falsehoods and delusions. The delusional parent has no choice but to reprogram the child into sharing the parent's delusions, otherwise the child may somehow contact the abandoned parent. To prevent this from happening, the abducting parent must isolate the child and fabricate a totally new reality for the child. How can anyone believe this is for the child's best interest?

It is easier to prevent an abduction than to get your child returned. This is especially true with international abductions. If you have reason to believe there is a risk of abduction, contact your attorney and police officials immediately. You need advice and resources in place to prevent an abduction and you need to know how to respond if an abduction occurs. The advice you receive will be very complex. There are attorneys and organizations that specialize in abduction response and prevention; you can find them on the Internet.

The United States and many countries have signed what is called the Hague Convention, which helps clearly define the protection of children.

If you have reason to believe an abduction is possible, there are actions you should take or that must be considered along with your attorney's advice.

- Always have in your possession recent color photographs of your children. The photos should not be more than a year old. Take new photographs if your child changes hair style.
- Have the local police department take fingerprints and a DNA sample of your child. Don't say to your child that you are doing this because you fear an abduction. Instead, calmly say to your child that this is a safety precaution recommended by police departments. You or your child may have seen on television occasions when the local police department had fingerprinting drives at the mall or community center.

- If the child has a passport, have someone trustworthy secure the passport. If the child has a dual citizenship, retaining a US passport may not be much help. It is easier to take a child out of the United States than it is to return them to the United States.
- Keep a record of names, addresses, and phone numbers of family members or the other parent's close friends.
- Gather information about resources that specialize in abduction response and prevention. There are both domestic and international resources. (Resources are not offered here because I cannot imply that I am making a specific recommendation of an organization without a thorough investigation, on a case-by-case basis. The Internet will direct you to resources.)

To give you an example of the complexities of responding to an abduction, consider your choices about how to coordinate all the activities needed and the decisions to be made:

- Reporting the abduction.
- Gathering needed information for the authorities.
- Finding the qualified attorney to coordinate legal activities.
- Identifying community and state resources such as Amber Alert.
- Finding persons of support.
- Managing the media, TV, press releases, and radio interviews.
- Distributing photographs.
- Financing the search.
- Preparation for reunification.

This list is only a sample of all you would need to consider if faced with an abduction. Imagine having to do all of this while coping with your emotions—worrying about your child and containing your rage toward the abducting parent. You can see that you would need help.

Pets

You may question why a book on parental alienation discusses pets. The number of households having pets is unknown. What is known is that the dog and cat population in the United States exceeds the capacity of our society to care for them. For the fortunate dogs and cats, they have had a stable and loving home threatened by a divorce or separation. For many parents, the dog or cat is a family member, loved by all, especially the children. A pet's ascension into the family fold may be difficult to navigate as families disassemble after a divorce or separation. Children can feel lured to stay with the parent who has the ability to care for the family pet. Sometimes an alienating parent, perhaps wanting to sooth their guilt, will promise the child a pet if he or she will live with them. Avoid offering this temptation. You could be asking for more trouble than you want.

Family members may view their pets as children and become very protective when time with and care of the pet is challenged. Custody of the pet can become symbolic of power, the one thought to be the more loving parent, or a means of keeping the remnants of the family together. Pets should not be a bargaining chip with the children.

Some courts are encouraging divorcing couples to be very explicit in the divorce agreements about pet visitation and expenses. Even cremation for pets can be difficult to navigate as divorcing parties may have a desire to each retain their beloved pet's remains. It is essential for estranged couples to be mindful of the impact their behavior has on family pets.

Tornado and Blizzard's Story

"We both wanted to spend time with Tornado and Blizzard, our canine children, and were afraid that the divorce would cause them to be confused as they would be living between two houses and two people who love them and wanted what was best for them. The court system recommended that we write our custody arrangements for them in our dissolution agreement, as pets are often battled over. We just wanted what was best for their futures."

The couple worked out an agreement that each share time with the family pets while the other is working. They share the financial responsibilities that are written in the dissolution papers.

Finding a Competent Reunification Therapist

There are no specific qualifications for a qualified reunification therapist. There is no certification program or a consensus as to what constitutes a qualified therapist. Reading this book alone does not make a therapist qualified. You should look for an independently licensed mental health professional who is respected by your local court, is knowledgeable of family law in your state, has had experience treating high-conflict families, understands and accepts the reality that PA and PAS exist, and expresses a commitment for long-term therapy if necessary. Frequently your attorney, along with the opposing attorney, will come up with a therapist for your approval. Be sure that none of the parties has any prior personal or professional relationship with the therapist.

If asked to submit a name of a therapist, you can ask a friend who may know the name of a therapist that they liked, ask the court's bailiff for a name, or a local professional association. After getting a couple of names, do not hesitate to call the therapist and ask questions about their qualifications. Do not start talking about the particulars of your case. This is not the time or place. The therapist does not want to hear you trying to convince him or her about the merits of your case. The therapist must be impartial if they accept your case. If you spend too much time describing your case to the prospective therapist, that therapist could be disqualified by the court because you have a prior relationship with the therapist, implying that the therapist will have a bias and will not be impartial. You may want your attorney to interview the prospective therapist if the therapy is going to be court ordered.

Custody

Joint custody, split custody, and shared parenting are confusing for many parents involved in custody litigation. Each jurisdiction may have different definitions or criteria for deciding the custody arrangements. To make the best decision for you and your children, you need to consult with your attorney. There is evidence [from a meta-analysis of studies (Bauserman 2002) comparing a child's adjustment in joint physical, joint legal, and paternal custody with intact families] that children in joint and legal custody were better adjusted than children living with a parent having sole custody. There was no difference in the children's adjustment compared with children in an intact family. This was not always true for children exposed to high conflict between the parents. Many courts will not consider joint custody when the parents are unable to control their anger or work together for the children's best interest. Though the court's rationale is understandable, knowing how the court feels about joint custody under these circumstances gives a parent an incentive to sabotage the relationship with the other parent. This is another way for an obsessed parent to manipulate the court.

Tip: A parent who is the child's gatekeeper and abuses the privilege should not be the custodial parent.

These are only a few of the issues that can come up during a contentious divorce. Addressing every contingency is not possible in this forum. Parents frequently write that their story is unique, unlike anyone else's. This may be true but for the most part, there are more similarities than differences. Any way you look at it, alienation is damaging and painful for all and must be prevented or stopped. There is no good excuse for anyone knowingly damaging a healthy and loving relationship with the children. This is abusive and should not be rewarded with custody.

12

When All Else Fails:
Seeking a Change in Custody

"I have tried everything and nothing seems to help"

The decision to seek custody should not be made lightly. Let us assume that after much quiet contemplation, you have come up with many reasons for going to court. You are sincere in your conviction that your children are better off living with you. You probably find it hard to imagine how the court could possibly disagree with your reasoning. In your heart, you know that if you can get your message across to the court, you will triumph and custody will be yours. And maybe you are right.

However, before getting too excited about your good intentions, you need a word of caution. You cannot assume that someone who understands your arguments will necessarily agree with you. Believing that you are the more competent parent and better suited to raise your children may have little bearing on what the court believes is in the child's best interest. You have to keep this sobering fact in mind before returning to court.

If you do decide to proceed, ask your attorney's advice. He or she knows your local court and can advise you on the strength of your case. Do not take offense if your attorney tells you that your chances are slim. He or she may be giving you good advice, even if you do not like what you are being told. If you insist on proceeding with the litigation, your attorney will follow your instructions or refer you to another attorney.

Before deciding to seek custody, try to anticipate the risks for both you and your children if you proceed with your case and lose. Begin by reminding yourself that your children did not ask for the divorce. There is the risk that you and your children could be worse off than before going to court. Whether you win or lose, what will be left of your relationship with your ex-spouse and the children? Maybe the cooperation you are now getting won't be there after the litigation because your ex-spouse will become bitter and angry. Take a moment and think twice about what is good for your children before you think about what is good for you. Courts do not like to upset your children's routines or stability unless there are very good reasons.

Gathering Information

"Would you find your father's old cell phone? I need to know who is in his address book."

Only the most severely alienated child will ask to go to court. For the most part, children want to avoid court and should be not be there unless asked by the attorney or the judge. To strengthen the parent's arguments for custody, he or she may ask the children to gather information to shore up their case. Sometimes, a parent's motivation for having children gather information is not very noble. A noncustodial parent struggling to pay bills may want to know how his ex-spouse is spending his money. Or the custodial parent may have reason to believe that their ex-spouse is hoarding money rather then paying a fair share of child support.

Tip: Asking your children to gather information about the other parent is alienating and should not occur.

Drinking and driving, excessive punishment, allowing the children to engage in dangerous activities, or failure to supervise are all reasons for parents to want their children to keep secrets because they know that some courts can restrict or even ban visits. Children should not be used in this manner because the message your child is receiving is that there is something desperately wrong with the targeted parent. This is alienation.

Tip: Children should not attend court unless asked by one of the attorneys or the judge. Attorneys should think twice before asking the children to appear in court.

For a parent to prove an allegation, they often need the children's cooperation to gather information about when and where questionable activities occur. Keep in mind that proving alienation does not guarantee that you will win custody. A parent may think that if he or she can prove to the court that their ex-spouse is mistreating or neglecting, they can get a court order to restrict visits to daytime hours or eliminate them altogether. Targeted parents may believe they will get custody. Parents may believe the end justifies the means because they are so intent on restricting or eliminating parenting time or getting custody.

The soliciting parent puts the children in a painfully awkward position because the children are asked to betray the other parent's trust. For example, a mother asks the children whether or not their father is having his girlfriend spend the night. If the allegation is true, and the children are not bothered by the practice, the mother may unintentionally cause her own estrangement. On the other hand, if the children are upset by the girlfriend's presence, the children may start feeling estranged from their father. Having to feed their mother information about their father's activities only adds to their discomfort. Even younger children learn that mother's inquiry has more significance than just satisfying curiosity.

Before deciding to gather information, ask yourself, "Why do I need this information?" Is the information pertinent for a parental or ex-spousal issue? If the information has more to do with an ex-spousal issue than the children's welfare, do not expect your children to gather information.

Parents may have a strong opinion about the use of drugs. No reasonable person can deny that certain drugs are illegal, and children should not be exposed to their use. Exposing children to drugs will cause most courts to ban parenting time entirely. However, there are those who believe marijuana should be legal and will smoke a "joint" in front of their children. They see nothing wrong with this practice, except they will ask the children to lie and not let anyone know what they are doing. These parents do not understand the dilemma in which they are placing the children. Again, the children become confused about how they should behave and where to place their loyalties. What values is the child learning?

Tip: Asking your children to keep secrets is alienating.

Drinking is a more complex issue, because it is a legal activity. A parent cannot expect the court to restrict a legal activity unless it has been shown that the drinker has behaved irresponsibly in the children's presence. What the parent does when the children are not present is no one's business, unless that activity is illegal or is a potential threat to their children's safety.

In recent years, smoking has become an issue for some parents. Recently on CNN a psychiatrist was saying that a popular singer was abusing her son because she was smoking in his presence and exposing him to second-hand smoke. Many may agree with the psychiatrist but smoking is legal and unless the judge orders otherwise, parents can smoke. There are courts that have ordered parents to not smoke in their child's presence because of ill health. I have heard of a court-ordered changing of custody because the parent refused to not smoke in their child's presence. If a child has documented evidence that he or she is allergic to cigarette smoke and the parent continues to smoke (or allows visitors to smoke), the parent is risking losing custody.

Try mediation or counseling to resolve any problems with your ex-spouse before returning to court. Going through any litigation, whether criminal or civil, is extremely stressful and emotionally draining for everyone, including your children. It makes no difference whether you are the plaintiff or defendant. You learn from your experience to avoid litigation if at all possible. Very often, there are no winners.

Are You Acting on Your Children's Behalf or Your Own?

You may not want to admit that your reasons for seeking custody are flawed. Your reasons may have more to do with ex-spousal issues than what is best for your children. This realization can be painful and difficult to accept. There are probably many arguments that you could list that would support your belief that you should have custody. To better understand how relevant your arguments may appear before the court, complete the following exercise.

Exercise: Why Are You Seeking Custody?

Write down all the reasons the court should award you custody of your children. Make the list as extensive as possible. After completing your list, review each item and place an "M" next to the items that reflect the reasons the change of custody would be good for you. Examples may include not having to pay child support or spending more time with the children.

Again review your list, this time placing a "C" next to the items that describe your reasons why a change of custody would be good for your children. Some examples may include "I'm home every day when my children return home from school; my neighborhood has younger children; or my children will not be exposed to drugs." Discriminating between an "M" and a "C" item is difficult and requires absolute honesty.

After completing your review of the items, you should have more "C" items than "M" items. The "C" items are the arguments that you would use to gain custody because they reflect the reasons living with you is good for your children. Typically, the court will have little interest in your "M" items even though you may have strong feelings about them. There may have been reasons that you believe are best for both you and your child. This could very well be true but again the court will focus more on what is best for your children and not what is good for you.

The "Best Interest of the Child" Doctrine

States have their own variations of how they define and interpret the "best interest of the child" doctrine. Though the state doctrine may be specific, judges will rely on their own interpretation of the law. Judge Leven said it well: "No one can really define 'best interest' to take in all the contingencies that may come before the court. There is no way of really defining it." He further explained "that the law places the burden on me to see to it that the child receives love, care, affection, proper parenting, and companionship [parenting time or visitation]." He is quick to tell parents, "I can't give that to your children. Since I can't, it is the parents' responsibility to do so. I expect them to do it. If they don't do it, I become extremely, extremely disappointed." Judge Leven believes there is no good definition for best interests, therefore his statement described his personal criteria for deciding custody. This is true for many judges and magistrates.

It is impractical for this book to outline all the state laws and various local interpretations of the best-interest doctrine. To give you some idea of what judges are looking for prior to making their decision, I have paraphrased criteria used by some states to give you some idea about what courts use for defining best interest. Some states have no specific criteria. You have to ask your attorney how your state defines best interest.

- The parents' wishes.
- The children's wishes. This is the reason why alienation (that is, both parents jockeying for their child's loyalty) is a vital issue.
- The child's interaction and relationship with his parents, siblings, and any other person who may significantly affect the child's best interest.
- The child's adjustment to his home, school, and community.
- The mental and physical health of both parents.
- The parent more likely to honor and encourage parenting time, or companionship rights approved by the court. Contrary to this criterion is parental alienation.

- Whether either parent has continuously and willfully denied the other parent his or her right to parenting time.

- Whether the noncustodial parent has failed to make all child support payments, including arrears, that are pursuant to a child support order.

- Whether either parent has been convicted of or pleaded guilty to any criminal offense involving any act that resulted in a child being abused or neglected, or whether either parent previously has been convicted of or pleaded guilty to any offense involving a victim who at the time was a member of the family or household and who caused physical harm to the victim in the commission of the offense.

- Whether either parent has or intends to establish a residence outside this state.

You will need to consult your local attorney to learn the specific laws or criteria for your state.

Issues to Consider before Pursuing Custody

You may feel ambivalent when you hear your children say, "I want to live with you." You may be excited by the compliment, and yet overwhelmed by the thought of the responsibility and lifestyle changes. Logistically, you may foresee many problems. You may not have a babysitter or adequate space. Living in an undesirable neighborhood for raising children could cause concern. While you gingerly inquire about your children's reasons, you imagine how your ex-spouse will feel when he or she hears the news.

There are several points to consider before making up your mind on what to do next. When you ask your children where they want to live, they may lie and say what they think you want to hear. They do not mean to be malicious. Rather, they do not want to hurt anyone's feelings. Often their stated desire to live with a parent is their way of saying, "I want Mommy and Daddy back together." This is particularly true with younger children. The children's fantasy that somehow their parents will reconcile is persistent, even with teenagers. Even when one parent has already remarried, the children often express the hope that one day their parents will again be back together.

Do not consider seeking a change of custody unless your children initiate the request or you have good reason to believe that remaining with their other parent seriously jeopardizes your children's welfare. If you are motivated because of neglect or physical or sexual abuse, you will need strong documentation from children service workers or some other independent collaboration. Your word or beliefs will not be enough to convince the court.

> Tip: If you initiate the idea to your children for a change of custody, you cannot trust that your children will be honest with you.

When thinking about a change of custody, you must move slowly. Remember, the best decisions are made when you have the maximum information. If you do not have all the information needed, postpone making a decision until later. There are times when the only decision that can be made at the moment is to decide what information needs to be gathered before making a later decision. This is true when considering seeking custody of your children. You need to think about the consequences your actions will have on everyone, including yourself. If you are unsuccessful in your bid for custody, you will have spent a lot of money and risked damaging your relationship with your ex-spouse. This could be an expensive price to pay for a long-shot.

Before announcing your intentions to your ex-spouse or especially to your children, consult your attorney. Learn about the laws for changing custody and the workings of your local court. Remember, it is the court, and not your children that decide custody. Try to get an idea from your attorney about the likelihood of whether you will be successful in getting custody. In many jurisdictions, it is nearly impossible to get an involuntary change of custody, which means both your children and your ex-spouse object, unless there is a legal provision for the children to choose where they want to live or there is evidence of abuse or neglect. Otherwise, you must prove to the court that your children's best interest is served by their living with you. This usually involves you having to publicly degrade or attack your ex-spouse to support your argument. Successfully attacking your ex-spouse's capacity to adequately parent is difficult. Typically, courts are justifiably biased in the belief that your children are better off remaining with the custodial parent to preserve the child's stability.

Do not make any promises to your children about changing custody. If your ex-spouse fights your attempt to gain custody, the time it takes in some jurisdictions to change custody can exceed one year. Your attorney can give you a better idea about how long the process may take if the change of custody is contested. Even if you feel confident telling your children, "After today's hearing you will come to live with me," do not make promises you cannot keep. Often cases are continued when the court realizes that a full hearing is needed to settle the case. Even after the judge hears the testimony, it may take days or even weeks to make a decision.

Courts frequently schedule many hearings at the same time because they know that many of the scheduled cases will be settled through negotiation rather than having a full hearing. When negotiations between the attorneys fail, the court many reschedule the hearing date rather than proceeding with the hearing. As a result, you and your children may wait, possibly for weeks or months, for another court date.

After talking with your attorney, you may raise the question to your ex-spouse about seeking a change of custody. True, your ex-spouse may feel hurt and angry, but it is better for you to raise the issue rather than having your children do the dirty work. The issue is between you and your ex-spouse rather then between the children and their other parent. Do not have your children be the harbinger of bad news. If you are afraid to talk to your ex-spouse about a change of custody, think about how your children will feel. There are also great risks if you later blind-side your ex-spouse with your intentions by unexpectedly having papers served at his or her place of work.

When you hear for the first time that your ex-spouse is seeking custody, do not drill your children for answers about where they want to live and why. Keep your composure. Reassure your children of your love while making no harsh declarations about what you are planning to do. Take time to calm down and consult your attorney to learn the best course of action. The attorney will advise you what to do next.

Natasha's Story

Natasha was a bubbly six-year-old who described how her father, Dan, would ask her where she wanted to live. Dan was concerned because he believed that Natasha's mother was neglectful. Often Natasha was filthy and unkempt. During Natasha's interview, she explained how she felt when Dad asked her where she wanted to live: "When he asks me that, I kinda feel I love my mom." She responds to her dad by saying "I don't know."

Natasha's statement reflects what often happens when a parent asks a child where he or she wants to live. Natasha felt uncomfortable with her father's questions. In response, she pulled away emotionally from her father and drew closer to her mother. Natasha's statement is a good example of the risk a parent takes when asking the children where they want to live. The parent asking the child may provoke the child's anxiety, causing the child to withdraw. I have talked to many children who have learned to dread going on parenting time because they are nagged about where they want to live. Parents insisting on asking where their child wants to live are only hurting themselves.

The circumstances at the time you decide to seek custody may determine the chances of your success. If you are seeking custody before the divorce, your chances of success are better than if you seek a change after the divorce is final. Your child's wishes can make a difference about your chances of success. Your circumstances may influence how you proceed.

Before the Divorce: You versus Your Spouse

You each enter the court arena equally entitled to the custody of your children before the custody has been granted. You will have the opportunity to present evidence and testimony about why it is in your children's best interest to live with you. Though the criteria for best interest is not always clear, each judge will have personal beliefs about how he or she will make the decision. For this reason, hire an attorney who knows and understands the biases in your local court. Outside attorneys are often not familiar with the local judge's biases or the workings of the court. Your attorney's lack of knowledge can work against you.

After the Divorce: You versus Your Ex-spouse and Children

You want to seek a change of custody but both your children and ex-spouse object. This is what I referred to as an involuntary change of custody. Seeking a change of custody under these circumstances is difficult if not impossible. You are asking the court to grant you custody when everyone, including your children, does not want the change to occur. The burden of proof is on you to show the court that it is in the children's best interest to live with you. Many courts have a bias that children are better off staying where they are if they are doing well in school, have a wide circle of friends, and are well-behaved. Changing custody means taking the risk of jeopardizing your children's good adjustment. Most often, parents seeking custody under these circumstances are motivated by ex-spousal issues and not the betterment of the children. Judges are aware of this and are sometimes suspicious of a parent's motives when they want a change of custody contrary to the wishes of the children.

Before the court will change custody, two issues will have to be addressed. First, you must prove to the court that your ex-spouse is somehow not suited to raise your children. The issue is not if you are a better parent but, instead, if the custodial parent is a bad parent. Most states do not have laws that define good parenting, but there is usually a law defining abusive or neglectful parenting. Each state or legal jurisdiction may have its own criteria for defining abuse or neglect. You will need to consult your attorney or local child protection agency to learn more about how your state defines abuse or neglect. Sometimes the information can be found on the Internet.

Courts are equally concerned about how cohabitation, homosexuality, drug and alcohol abuse, or other deviations from community standards of proper conduct will influence your children's adjustment and welfare. Though the issues are not considered abuse or neglect, they are concerns for some courts that may influence the decision for an involuntary change of custody. Jurisdictions will vary on the importance they place on these issues. Judges and magistrates have their biases. For example, courts in smaller towns tend to worry more about cohabitation than courts in larger, more liberal cities.

It is not enough for you to show the court that a parent's behavior may be neglectful, abusive, or contrary to community standards. You may have to demonstrate to the court how your children have been harmed by the custodial parent's alleged misconduct. For example, your ex-spouse may be a homosexual. Are you able to prove to the court that your ex-spouse's sexual orientation is harmful to your children? The fact that you believe that a homosexual lifestyle is harmful or contrary to your values is not a strong enough argument to convince most courts to make an involuntary change of custody, unless the court shares your bias or the other parent behaves in an offensive manner in your children's presence. There is no supporting evidence to suggest that living with a homosexual parent is inherently harmful or damaging to children.

If you are successful in convincing the court that your ex-spouse is neglectful or abusive or behaves in a manner potentially harmful to your children, the second issue before the court is, "Who shall care for your children?" Your answer of course is, "I will." Now your task is to convince the court that you are right for the job. The court may still not agree with your argument. Instead, it may require a custody evaluation or an independent investigation by the guardian *ad litem* before deciding on a change of custody. This process can be expensive and time-consuming.

After the Divorce: You and Your Young Children versus Your Ex-spouse

You and your children want you to seek a change of custody but your ex-spouse objects. Some states have a provision in the law to allow a child at a certain age to address the court and express their preference as to where they want to live. The specific age of election is stated in the state law though many states are getting away from this practice. The rationale for the age of election is based on the state's judgment that children at a certain age, say 14 or 15, should have sufficient maturity to make a responsible choice. In recent years, legislators have been questioning whether the election law is a good idea because of the burden that the decision puts on the children. In effect, the election laws are asking the children to publicly reject one of their parents. Most would agree that this cannot be good for children. Rather than election, courts still want to give the children the option to express their preference, but the court reserves the right to make the decision based on the best-interest doctrine. In this way, the children and parents should understand that it isn't the children who make the decision but the courts. I believe this is a better arrangement for the children. They shouldn't have to bear the burden of facing a parent whom they have just publicly rejected.

As the noncustodial parent with children under the age of election, you are faced with the same issues as the parent who is seeking custody where neither the children nor the other parent want the change. You must show the court how the custodial parent has been abusive, neglectful, or behaved in a manner that is detrimental to your children's welfare. You must also show the court why it is in your children's best interest to reside with you. Only then do you have a chance for success. Generally, your chance of success is poor under these circumstances also.

After Divorce: You and Your Teenagers versus Your Ex-spouse

You and your teenager want you to seek a change of custody but your ex-spouse objects. All the children are older or over the age of election. Depending upon your children's ages, the judge will seriously consider their preference as to where they want to live. The judge may talk with your children in his chambers so they can share their feelings without feeling intimidated by their parents' and attorneys' presence. The judge will try to determine if your children have been pressured by either parent, evaluate the child's maturity, and try to understand their reasons for wanting to live with the chosen parent. Reasons such as "My dad lets me stay up late," "I can date whoever I want," or "My dad will buy me whatever I want," do not reflect much maturity and probably will not help to influence the court. Judges will listen for more mature motivations such as "I can tell my dad how I feel," "I love both of my parents but I want to get to know my father better," or "I'm more comfortable with my mom."

Each judge will weigh the children's motivations differently. Some are more liberal in supporting the children's choice. He or she may believe that children of a certain age are old enough to know what they want. Other judges will place greater importance on wanting to maintain stability in the children's lives, especially if they appear well-adjusted.

If you know that your children want to live with their other parent and you object, your task may be to show the court why your children's wishes should not be granted. You may need to show the court that the change of custody is not in the children's best interest. In many courts, this is difficult to accomplish.

You and One Child versus Your Ex-spouse and Another Child

You and one of your two children want a change of custody but your ex-spouse objects. The change of custody requires splitting the children. Courts do not like splitting children between their two parents because of their belief that children are better off together. Parents must convince the court that splitting is best for the children and will not cause them harm. The judge may interview the children, together or separately, to learn how they feel about the proposal. If the children have the slightest reservation about living in separate homes, the court will usually deny the parent's request. Courts are biased in wanting to keep children together so they have the opportunity to have a sibling relationship.

You and Your Ex-spouse versus the Children

You and your ex-spouse want a change of custody but the children want to remain with the original custodial parent. Parents occasionally decide between themselves to change their children's residence without informing the court or seeking a formal change of custody. Unless someone complains, the court will not know where the children are living. In this situation, the children will remain wherever the parents decide.

When both parents agree on changing custody, the court will typically support their decision. Both attorneys will document the parents' approval with the parents' signatures on a written motion before the court. The court will document the consent with the judge's signature on the motion. A formal hearing before the court is usually not necessary provided both parties agree to the change of custody and provisions for child support.

When both parents agree to a change of custody, the children usually have little, if anything, to say about the decision. If the court somehow learns of the children's opposition to their parents' request, the court may assign the children a guardian *ad litem* to assure protection of their rights and best interest.

You can see that changing custody is a complex issue with many ramifications. The decision should not be taken lightly. Do not make threats to change custody toward your ex-spouse during a fit of anger. Also, do not expect your attorney to be your therapist during these trying times. You naturally want your attorney's support for what you decide but attorneys have their professional boundaries. You need to respect their privacy and work schedule. You hired your attorney for a professional service and not to be your friend.

.

Postscript

I hope that you have found *Beyond Divorce Casualties* helpful. If there is one message central to this volume, it is that you can only control your own behavior, not that of your child's other parent. You must take responsibility for your own behavior, first and foremost, and you will see changes for the better in your relationship with your child and maybe even, with time, the other parent. This book provides many tools to help you in this journey. Good luck in the road ahead.

Appendix:
Parental Alienation Inventory

Dr. William Bernet (2010) has done an exemplary job compiling research and writing a soon to-be-published book arguing for the inclusion of parental alienation disorder in the upcoming DSM-V. The outcome of his efforts is not known but his arguments and documentation are very compelling. His proposal for the diagnosis is different than what I have described in this book. *Beyond Divorce Casualties* makes a distinction between parental alienation and parental alienation syndrome. The argument for the distinction is that the treatments for the victimized child and the parents are different, though both child and parents have to be involved in the treatment or reunification. Dr. Bernet rightfully takes the position that parental alienation disorder is a relationship problem that involves both parents and the child. His argument, if accepted by the DSM Task Force, would not negate the contribution of this book outlining various approaches for reunification.

Regarding the terminology used in DSM-V, Dr. Bernet concludes that parental alienation can be conceptualized as either a "mental disorder" or a "relational problem" (a V-code). If parental alienation were adopted as a mental disorder, it might be placed in the DSM-V appendix, "Criteria Sets and Axes for Further Study." If parental alienation were adopted as a relational problem, it would be included in the DSM-V chapter, "Other Conditions That May Be a Focus of Clinical Attention." A parent-child relational problem already exists in the DSM-IV-TR (2000). Dr. Bernet is advocating that the parental alienation relational problem be a stand-alone diagnosis or, at minimum, be specifically defined as an example of a severe parent-child relational problem.

The words *parental alienation* must be published in the DSM-V to receive the recognition the diagnosis deserves and to quiet many of the critics that have politicized the words. This issue must get resolved so mental health professionals and the legal community can get beyond the politics and get on with helping children and families. Dr. Bernet states, "Parental alienation disorder should be the diagnosis if the child's symptoms are persistent enough and severe enough to meet the criteria for that disorder." Dr. Bernet has taken Dr. Gardner's (1998) criteria for parental alienation syndrome and adapted them to his proposed diagnosis. The strength of the proposed criteria is that the diagnosis takes into account that there will be various severities of the disorder. All the criteria are not needed to make the diagnosis. Dr. Gardner did not make this clear in his writings.

Diagnostic Criteria for Parental Alienation Disorder

A. The child—usually one whose parents are engaged in a high-conflict divorce—allies himself or herself strongly with one parent and rejects a relationship with the other, alienated parent without legitimate justification. The child resists or refuses contact or parenting time with the alienated parent.
B. The child manifests the following behaviors:
    (1) a persistent rejection or denigration of a parent that reaches the level of a campaign;
    (2) weak, frivolous, and absurd rationalizations for the child's persistent criticism of the rejected parent.
C. The child manifests two or more of the following six attitudes and behaviors:
    (1) lack of ambivalence;
    (2) independent-thinker phenomenon;
    (3) reflexive support of one parent against the other;
    (4) absence of guilt over exploitation of the rejected parent;
    (5) presence of borrowed scenarios;
    (6) spread of the animosity to the extended family of the rejected parent.
D. The duration of the disturbance is at least two months.
E. The disturbance causes clinically significant distress or impairment in social, academic (occupational), or other important areas of functioning.
F. The child's refusal to have contact with the rejected parent is without legitimate justification. That is, parental alienation disorder is not diagnosed if the rejected parent maltreated the child.

References

Amato, P. R. 1993. Children's adjustment to divorce: theories, hypothesis, and empirical support. *Journal of Marriage and the Family* 55: 23–38.

Amato, P. R. and Rezac, S. 1994. Contact with residential parents, interpersonal conflict, and children's behavior. *Journal of Family Issues* 15: 191–207.

American Psychiatric Association. 1968. *Diagnostic and statistical manual II for mental disorder*, 2nd ed. Washington, D.C.: American Psychiatric Association.

American Psychiatric Association. 1987. *Diagnostic and statistical manual III for mental disorder*, 3rd ed. Washington, D.C.: American Psychiatric Association.

American Psychiatric Association. 2000. *Diagnostic and statistical manual IV-TR for mental disorder*, 4th ed. Washington, D.C.: American Psychiatric Association.

American Psychological Association. 1994. Guidelines for child custody evaluations in divorce proceedings. *American Psychologist* 49: 677–680.

American Psychological Association. 2002. Ethical principles of psychologists and code of conduct. *American Psychologist* 58: 377–402.

Arnold, K. D. and Sherrill, J. D. 1998. Directed family counseling: structured treatment for conflicted divorcing families. *Ohio Psychologists* June: 13–17.

Association of Family and Conciliation Courts: Task Force on Parenting Coordination. 2006. Guidelines for parenting coordination. *Family Court Review* 44 (1): 164–181.

Baker, A. J. L. 2007. *Adult children of parental alienation syndrome: Breaking the ties that bind*. New York: The Norton Professional Book.

Baker, A. J. L. and Darnall, D. 2006. Behaviors and strategies employed in parental alienation: A survey of parental experiences. *Journal of Divorce and Remarriage* 45 (1/2): 97–124.

Baker, A. J. L. and Darnall, D. 2007. A construct study of the eight symptoms of severe parental alienation syndrome: A survey of parental experiences. *Journal of Divorce and Remarriage* 47 (1/2): 55–76.

Bala, N. and Schuman, J. 2000. Allegations of sexual abuse when parents have separated. *Canadian Family Law Quarterly* 17: 191–241.

Barker, R. L. 1995. *The social work dictionary*. Washington, D.C.: National Association of Social Workers Press.

Barris, M. A., Coats, C. A., Duvall, B. B., Garrity, C. B., Johnson, E. T., and LaCrosse, E. R. 2001. *Working with high-conflict families of divorce: A guide for professionals*. Northvale, N.J.: Jason Aronson.

Bauserman, R. 2002. Child adjustment in joint-custody versus sole-custody arrangements: A meta-analytic review. *Journal of Family Psychology* 16 (1): 91–102.

Bennett, B. E., Bricklin, P. M., Harris, E., Knapp, S., VandeCreek, L., and Younggren, J. N. 2006. *Assessing and managing risk in psychological practice.* Rockville, Md.: The Trust.

Berg, B. and Kelly, R. 1979. The measured self-esteem of children from broken, rejected, and accepted families. *Journal of Divorce* 2: 363–369.

Bernet, W. 2010. *Parental Alienation, DSM-V, and ICD-11.* Springfield, Ill.: Charles C Thomas Publishers.

Blank, G. K. and Ney, T. 2006. The de-construction of concept in divorce litigation: A discursive critique of "parental alienation syndrome" and "the alienated child." *Family Court Review* 44 (1): 135–148.

Bow, J. N., Gould, J. W., Flens, J. R., and Greehut, D. 2006. Testing in child custody evaluations—selection, usage, and Daubert admissibility: A survey of psychologists. *Journal of Forensic Psychology Practice* 6 (2): 17–38.

Braiker, B. and Dy, C. 2007. Just don't call me Mr. Mom. *Newsweek Magazine.* October 8.

Brandon, D. J. 2006. Can four hours make a difference? Evaluation of a parent education program for divorcing parents. *Journal of Divorce and Remarriage* 45(1/2): 171–185.

Bruch, C. S. 2001. Parental alienation syndrome and parental alienation: Getting it wrong in child custody cases. *Family Law Quarterly* 35(3): 527–552.

Campbell, T. 1992. Psychotherapy with children of divorce: The pitfalls of triangulated relationships. *Psychotherapy* 29 (4): 646–652.

Cassity, J. 1999. "The nature of the child's ties." In *Handbook of attachment: Theory, research, and clinical applications,* ed. J. Cassity and P. R. Shave, 3–20. New York: Guilford Press.

Ceci, S. J. and Bruck, M. 1995. *Jeopardy in the courtroom: A scientific analysis of children's testimony.* Washington, D.C.: American Psychological Association.

Chatav, Y. and Whisman, M. A. 2007. Marital dissolution and psychiatric disorders: An investigation of risk factors. *Journal of Divorce and Remarriage* 47(1/2): 1–13.

Clawar, S. S. and Rivlin, B. V. 1991. Children held hostage: Dealing with programmed and brainwashed children. Chicago, Ill.: *American Bar Association.*

Collaborative Divorce Newsblog. 2007. *American Bar Association Ethics Opinion Confirms Collaborative Law Is Ethical Mode of Practice* (October 31, 2007), http://www.collaborativedivorcenews.com/2007/10/american-ethics-opinion.

Cummings, E. M. and Davies, P. T. 1994. *Children and marital conflict.* New York: Guilford Press.

Darnall, D. C. 1993. The content validity of parental alienation. Unpublished raw data.

Darnall, D. C. 1998. *Divorce casualties: Protecting your children from parental alienation.* Dallas, Tx.: Taylor Publishing.

Darnall, D. C. 2008. *Divorce casualties: Understanding parental alienation.* Dallas, Tx.: Taylor Publishing.

Darnall, D. C. and Steinberg, B. F. 2008. Motivational models for spontaneous renunciation with the alienated child. *The American Journal of Family Therapy* 36(2): 107–115.

Darnall, D. C. and Steinberg, B. F. 2008. Motivational models for spontaneous renunciation with the alienated child: part II. *The American Journal of Family Therapy* 36 (3): 253–261.

Daubert v. Merrell Dow Pharmaceuticals, 509 U.S. 579, 113 S. Ct. 2786, 125.L.Ed. (2nd 469 1993).

Dunne, J. and Hedrick, M. 1994. The parental alienation syndrome: An analysis of sixteen selected cases. *Journal of Divorce and Remarriage* 21 (3/4): 21–38.

Eddy, B. 2006. *High-conflict people in legal disputes.* Janis Publications.

Ellis, A. and Dryden, W. 1996. *The Practice of Rational Emotive Therapy,* 2nd ed. New York, N.Y.: Springer Publishing.

Ellis, E. M. 2000. *Divorce wars: Interventions with families in conflict.* Washington, D.C.: American Psychological Association.

Emery, R. E. 1982. Interparental conflict and the children of discord and divorce. *Psychological Bulletin* 92: 310–330.

Epstein, N. B. and Baucom, D. H. 2002. *Enhanced cognitive-behavioral therapy for couples: A contextual approach.* Washington, D.C.: American Psychological Association.

Faller, K. and DeVoe, E. 1995. Allegations of sexual abuse in divorce. *Journal of Child Sexual Abuse* 4 (4): 1–25.

Farmer, R. F. and Chapman, A. L. 2008. *Behavioral interventions in cognitive behavior therapy.* Washington, D.C.: American Psychological Association.

Forehand, R., McCombs, A., Long, N., Brody, G., and Fauber, R. 1988. Early adolescent adjustment to recent parental divorce: The role of interparental conflict and adolescent sex as mediating variable. *Journal of Consulting and Clinical Psychology* 56 (4): 624–627.

Frye v. United States, 293 F. 1013 (D.C. Cir., 1923).

Gardner, R. A. 1985. Recent trends in divorce and custody litigation. *Academy Forum* 29 (2): 3–7.

Gardner, R. A. 1998. *Parental alienation syndrome,* 2nd ed. Cresskill, N.J.: Creative Therapeutics.

Gardner, R. A. 2001. Should courts order PAS children to visit/reside with the alienated parent?: A follow-up study. *The American Journal of Forensic Psychology* 19 (3): 61–106.

Gardner, R. A. 2002. Parental alienation syndrome vs. parental alienation: Which diagnosis should be used in child custody litigation? *American Journal of Family Therapy* 30 (2): 101–123.

Garrity, C. B. and Baris, M. A. 1994. *Caught in the middle: Protecting the children in high-conflict divorce.* New York: Lexington Books.

Gould, J. W. 1998. *Conducting scientifically crafted child custody evaluations.* Thousand Oaks, Cal.: Sage Publications.

REFERENCES

Gould, J. W., Martindale, D. A., and Eidman, M. H. 2007. Is parental sexual orientation probative in child custody advisory reports?: It depends! *Journal of Forensic Psychological Practice* 7 (4): 111–124.

Grych, J. H. and Fincham, F. D. 1992. Interventions for children of divorce: Towards greater integration of research and action. *Psychology Bulletin* 111 (3): 434–454.

Guidubaldi, J., Perry, J., and Nastasi, B. K. 1987. Assessment and intervention for children of divorce: Implications of the NASP-KSU nationwide study. *Advances in Family Intervention, Assessment, and Theory* 4: 33–69.

Gunsberg, L. and Hymowitz, P. 2005. *The handbook of divorce and custody: Forensic, developmental and clinic perspectives.* Hillsdale, N.J.: The Analytic Press.

Herman, S. 2005. Improving decision making in forensic child sexual abuse evaluations. *Law and Human Behavior* 29 (1): 87–120.

Hetherington, E. M., ed. 1999. *Coping with divorce, single parenting, and remarriage: A risk and resiliency perspective.* Mahwah, N.J.: Erlbaum.

Hetherington, E. M., Cox, M., and Cox, R. 1985. Long-term effects of divorce and remarriage on the adjustment of children. *Journal of the American Academy of Child Psychiatry* 24: 518–530.

Hodges, W. F. and Bloom, B. L. 1984. Parent's report of children's adjustment to marital separation: A longitudinal study. *Journal of Divorce* 8 (1): 33–51.

Hoff, P. M. 1997. Parental kidnapping: Prevention and remedies. *Office of Juvenile Justice and Delinquency.* Washington, D.C.: U.S. Department of Justice.

Hoffman, D. 2007. American Bar Association ethics opinion confirms collaborative law is ethical mode of practice. *Collaborative Divorce Newsblog* (December 25, 2007), http://www.collaborativedivorcenews.com/2007/10/american-bar-association-ethics-opinion.

Jacobson, D. S. 1978. The impact of marital separation/divorce on children: II, Interparent hostility and child adjustment. *Journal of Divorce* 2 (1): 3–19.

Jamieson, C. D. 2007. *How to prepare a champagne case on a beer bottle budget.* Presented at Parental Alienation Awareness Organization conference.

Johnston. J. R., Kline, M., and Tschann, J. M. 1989. Ongoing post divorce conflict: Effects on children of joint custody and frequent access. *American Orthopsychiatric Association* 59 (4): 576–592.

Johnston, J. R., Walters, M. G., and Friedlander, S. 2001. Therapeutic work with alienated children and their families. *Family Court Review* 39 (3): 316–333.

Kelly, J. B. 2000. Children's adjustment in conflicted marriage and divorce: A decade review of research. *American Academy of Child and Adolescent Psychiatry* 39 (8): 963–973.

Kelly, J. B., and Johnson, J. R. 2001. The alienated child: A reformulation of parental alienation syndrome. *Family Court Review* 39 (3): 249–266.

Kriesberg, L. and Thorson, S. J. 1991. *Timing conditions, strategies, and errors: Introduction in timing the de-escalation of international conflicts.* Syracuse University Press, 1–24.

Kuehnle, K. and Drozd, L. 2005. *Child custody litigation: Allegations of child sexual abuse,* vol. 2. New York: Haworth Press.

REFERENCES

Lampel, A. 1986. Post-divorce therapy with high-conflict families. *The Independent Practitioner* 6 (3): 22–26.

Libby, L. K., Shaeffer, E. M., Eiback, R. P., and Slemmer, J. A. 2007. Picture yourself at the polls: Visual perspective in mental imagery affects self-perception and behavior. *Psychological Science* 18 (3): 199–203.

Long, N., Slater, E., Forehand, R., and Fauber, R. 1988. Continued high or reduced interparental conflict following divorce: Relation to young adolescent adjustment. *Journal of Consulting and Clinical Psychology* 56 (3): 467–469.

Mackey, W. C. and Immerman, R. S. 2007. Fatherlessness by divorce contrasted to fatherlessness by non-marital births: A distinction with a difference for the community. *Journal of Divorce and Remarriage* 47 (1/2): 111–134.

Miller, W. R. and Rollnick, S. 1991. *Motivational interviewing: Preparing people to change addictive behavior.* New York: Guilford Press.

Nichols, M. P. and Schwartz, R. C. 1998. *Family therapy: Concepts and methods*, 4th ed. Boston: Allyn and Bacon.

Petrich, D. K. 2008. *Project Hurricane D: Pet bereavement and families.* Unpublished doctoral dissertation, University of Akron, Ohio.

Pruitt, D. and Olczak, P. 1995. Beyond hope: Approaches to resolving seemingly intractable conflict. *Conflict, cooperation, and justice: Essays inspired by the work of Morton Deutsch*, ed. B. B. Bunker and J. Z. Rubin. New York: Sage.

Poole, D. A. and Lamb, M. E. 1998. *Investigative interviews of children.* Washington, D.C.: American Psychological Association.

Porter, B. and O'Leary, K. D. 1980. Marital discord and childhood behavior problems. *Journal of Abnormal Child Psychology* 80: 287–295.

Rothenberg, M. A. and Chapman, C. F. 2000. *Dictionary of medical terms for the nonmedical person*, 4th ed. Hauppauge, N.Y.: Barron's Educational Series.

Rubin, J. Z. 1991. The timing of ripeness and the ripeness of timing. *Introduction in timing the de-escalation of international conflicts*, ed. Louis Kriesberg and Stuard J. Thorson. Syracuse University Press, 237–246.

Sarrazin, J. and Cyr, F. 2007. Parental conflicts and their damaging effects on children. *Journal of Divorce and Remarriage* 47(1/2): 77–93.

Schepard, A. I. 2004. *Children, courts, and custody: Interdisciplinary models for divorcing families.* New York: Cambridge University Press.

Schmidt, F., Cuttress, L. J., Land, J., Lewandowski, M. J., and Rawana, J. S. 2007. Assessing the parent-child relationship in parenting capacity evaluations: Clinical applications of attachment research. *Family Court Review* 45 (2): 247–259.

Slater, E. J. and Haber, J. D. 1984. Adolescent adjustment following divorce as a function of familial conflict. *Journal of Consulting and Clinical Psychology* 52 (5): 920–921.

Sobell, L. C. and Sobell, M. B. 2003. Using motivational interviewing techniques to talk with clients about their alcohol abuse. *Cognitive and Behavioral Practice* 10: 214–221.

Sorensen, E. D. and Goldman, J. 1990. Custody determinations and child development: A review of the current literature. *Journal of Divorce* 13(4): 53–67.

REFERENCES

Stahl, P. M. 1999. *Complex issues in child custody evaluations.* Thousand Oaks, Cal.: Sage Publications.

Sullivan, M. J. and Kelly, J. B. 2001. Legal and psychological management of cases with an alienated child. *Family Court Review* 39 (3): 299–315.

Summers, D. M. and Summers, C. C. 2006. Unadulterated arrogance: Autopsy of the narcissistic parental alienator. *The American Journal of Family Therapy* 34: 399–428.

Tesler, P. H. and Thompson, P. 2006. *Collaborative divorce: The revolutionary new way to restructure your family, resolve legal issues, and move on with your life.* New York: Regan Books.

Tong, D. 2001. *Elusive innocence: Survival guide for the falsely accused.* Lafayette, La.: Huntington House Publishers.

Trocmé, N. and Bala, N. 2005. False allegations of abuse and neglect when parents separate. *Child Abuse and Neglect* 29: 1333–1345.

Turket, I. D. 1994. Child visitation interference in divorce. *Clinical Psychology Review* 14 (8): 737–742.

Ver Steegh, N. 2005. Differentiating types of domestic violence: Implication for child custody. *Louisiana Law Review* 65 (4): 1389–1431.

Visher, E. B. and Visher, J. S. 1982. *How to win as a step-family*, 2nd ed. New York: Brunner/Mazel.

Wade v. Hirschman, 903 So2d 928 (Florida Supreme Court 2005).

Waldron, K. H. and Joanis, J. D. 1996. Understanding and collaboratively treating parental alienation syndrome. *American Journal of Family Law* 10: 121–133.

Wallace, H. 2002. *Family violence: Legal, medical and social perspective.* Boston: Pearson Education.

Wallerstein, J. S. and Kelly, J. B. 1980. *Surviving the breakup: How children and parents cope with divorce.* New York: Basic Books.

Wallerstein, J. S. and Tanke, T. 1996. To move or not to move: Psychological and legal considerations in the relocation of children following divorce. *Family Law Quarterly* 30 (2): 305–332.

Warshak, R. A. 1999. *Parental alienation in the courts.* Dallas: Clinical Psychology Associates.

Warshak, R. A. 2001. *Divorce poison.* New York: Harper Collins.

Weitzman, J. 2004. Use of the one-way mirror in child custody reunification cases. *Journal of Child Custody* 1(4): 27–48.

West Virginia. 2008. *Crimes against the peace: Falsely reporting child abuse.* Chapter 61, article 6, §61: 6–25.

Wolpe, J. 1992. *The practice of behavior therapy*, 4th ed. New York: Allyn and Bacon.

Wood, C. L. 1994. The parental alienation syndrome: A dangerous aura of reliability. *Loyola of Los Angeles Law Review* 29: 1367–1415.

Zartman, W. I. 1989. *Ripe for resolution.* New York: Oxford University Press.

Zartman, W. I. and Johannes, A. 1991. "Power strategies to de-escalation." *Introduction in timing the de-escalation of international conflicts*, ed. Louis Kriesberg and Stuard J. Thorson. Syracuse University Press, 152–181.

Index

About the Author

Douglas Darnall, Ph.D., is a licensed psychologist and CEO of PsyCare, Inc., which has nine outpatient mental health clinics in northeastern Ohio and western Pennsylvania. He teaches workshops on parental alienation syndrome and divorce to the professional community. He has served as a consultant or an evaluator in hundreds of cases, testified in eleven states, and has appeared on Court TV, *The Montel Show,* and numerous radio shows. He has coauthored a number of peer-reviewed journal articles on parental alienation.